ADVANCE PRAISE FOR *DISRUPT OR DIE*

"I have often said if you want to sustain success, surround yourself with good people. I think one of Jed's strengths as a CEO is that he builds great teams and finds ways to challenge them and motivate them to excel. When I visited Delphix, I loved seeing the team Jed assembled and the culture he created. Jed has found a powerful formula for success, and this book will help others do the same."

—ROBERT KRAFT, Chairman and CEO, Kraft Group,
Owner of the New England Patriots

"The old saying that 'those who can, do, while those who can't, teach or write books' doesn't apply to Jed. He has a proven track record of bringing digital transformation to market. In this book, he teaches invaluable lessons and insights gleaned from the front lines of innovation."

—DAVID CHERITON, Professor Emeritus of Computer Science,
Stanford; Cofounder, Arista; First Investor, Google

"This is a fast-moving narrative on the digital imperative and how it sorts the winners and losers. Jed, a pur sang entrepreneur, has been in the digital arena a long time, has lived it, and has a good tale to tell!"

—FRANK SLOOTMAN, Chairman and Former CEO, ServiceNow

"Jed is an impressive CEO, visionary, executor, and technologist. *Disrupt or Die* unlocks Jed's strategy and techniques for leading in an age of rapid disruption. This is the digital playbook of our time."

—DAVID CASTELLANI, SVP and Business Information Officer,
New York Life

"Jed looks at the world in a way great people do, playing to serve others, finding ways to help people be their best. Jed finds where he needs to move before others see it. I liken him to Steph Curry. He makes phenomenal shots from farther than you think. This book passes you the ball and teaches you how. It's time to bring it!"

—RONNIE LOTT, Elected into NFL Hall of Fame,
Four-Time Super Bowl Champion, Venture Investor

"Jed has spilled Silicon Valley's magic beans in *Disrupt or Die*. Every CEO in the world needs to read this book."

—JYOTI BANSAL, Founding CEO, AppDynamics
(Acquired by Cisco for $3.7 billion)

"Jed is one of the few Silicon Valley entrepreneurs whom I always pay close attention to because of his insights into the future of business. This book is based on hundreds of top-level executive meetings Jed has had around the globe with *Fortune* 2000 companies as founder of Delphix—one of the most innovative startups in Silicon Valley. No other business book can claim as much research as Jed has made in writing this book."

—TOM FOREMSKI, Editor of the *Silicon Valley Watcher*

"With crowdfunding, angels, VCs, crossover funds, and corporate investors, startup funding is at an all-time high. If you run a legacy company or you're trying to disrupt one, you can't afford not to read this book."

—DAN SCHOLNICK, General Partner, Trinity Ventures

"Jed has been instrumental in creating disruptive technology, before the term *disruptive* became a mainstay. His vision and ability to execute is what makes his insights a must to succeed in the digital age."

—MARIVI STUCHINSKY, CTO, Farmers Insurance

"Whether you're an innovator at a startup or an established company, *Disrupt or Die* can save you thousands of hours of wasted work, hundreds of wrong decisions, ten years of wandering, and one case of extinction."

—ANDREW LI, Founder and CEO, BadData

"Jed's been a CEO multiple times. It shows in his wisdom and leadership. CEOs may be inspired to 'fire themselves' and reinvent their businesses after reading this book."

—JOE LONSDALE, Founding Partner, 8VC;
Cofounder of Palantir, Addepar, and OpenGov

"Jed is a passionate innovator with a shining intellect. His book is a must-read for anyone driving digital transformation. Read *Disrupt or Die* ... before it's too late."

—MILO SPRAGUE, CTO, Silicon Valley Bank

"I have never met anyone quite like Jed. When he decides to analyze something, you need not consult or look at any other source because you can rest assured he has left no stone unturned on the subject, as you'll learn reading *Disrupt or Die*. He is not only one of the most intelligent people I have ever worked with; he is also relentless in his desire to understand anything that he finds interesting, and digital transformation is interesting to the entire world."

—BARRY LIBENSON, Global CIO, Experian

"Jed is a serial entrepreneur, technology visionary, and developer of disruptive solutions that have helped transform IT organizations. At Molina Healthcare, a *Fortune* 150 company, Delphix products proved to be transformational as we tripled our business over three years."

—RICK HOPFER, CIO, Molina Healthcare

"*Disrupt or Die* will challenge everything you think you know about digital transformation and disruption."

—ED WALSH, General Manager, IBM Storage

"Jed is one of the few entrepreneurs whom I have backed twice. He melds complex technologies into products that create significant business impact for the largest enterprises."

—CHRIS SCHAEPE, Founding Partner, Lightspeed Venture Partners

"Jed is a digital visionary and accomplished entrepreneur, having founded both Avamar and Delphix. In *Disrupt or Die*, he provides us with a rich tapestry of high-impact ideas about innovation, building, and scaling in a highly readable and entertaining format."

—ASHEEM CHANDNA, Partner, Greylock Partners

"The rate of new technology adoption is increasing rapidly, putting traditional companies at great risk of disruption. *Disrupt or Die* helps CEOs navigate that risk."

—ROGER DICKEY, Founder and CEO, Gigster; Founder, Mafia Wars

"Jed didn't just write the book on digital disruption. He's lived it, first with data deduplication at Avamar and a second time with Delphix."

—KAYCEE LAI, President and COO, Waterline Data

"In *Disrupt or Die*, Jedidiah Yueh has provided us with a blueprint for harnessing the forces of the digital age. He manages to present contrarian perspectives on Silicon Valley dogma in a manner that is evidentially rich and thus easy to assimilate. Better still, he provides frameworks and rules to enable even the most risk averse in their pursuit of an 'Appzilla.'

"The book interweaves 'how to' pragmatism with his own extensive experience, which is built on the most unlikely of 'initial conditions.' His time-sensitive approach makes the book feel like an insider's guide to the history of Silicon Valley.

"Yueh is a highly credible guide for both startups and legacy players who are looking to become economically relevant in the digital age."

—ADE MCCORMACK, Digital Strategist and Author of *Biz 4.0: An Anthropological Blueprint for Business in the Digital Age*

"Just as the PBS series *Connections* peeled back the veil of history to show how the world has been influenced by a web of seemingly interconnected events, Jed goes beyond the first- or second-order consequences of change to help the reader understand the broad impact of digital disruption. You don't have to be a genius to lead in the digital world. You just need to see where others are blind. *Disrupt or Die* helps you see what's coming before it's too late."

—RALPH LOURA, CTO, Rodan + Fields

"Jed's innovations have generated billions in revenue, benefited tens of thousands of companies, and created thousands of jobs. Now, everyone will have a chance to learn from his visionary insights on how to drive digital transformation."

—CHAD CARDENAS, MANAGING Director, InstantScale Ventures

"Companies that do not take provocative steps to transform from 'born analogue' to 'transformed digital' will lose the ability to compete. Most digital strategies and playbooks are authored by consultants, analysts, and researchers—not actual practitioners. Jed has a successful track record for disrupting established technologies and industries. When he talks digital, we should all be listening."

—SCOTT SPRADLEY, CTO, Tyson Foods; former CIO, HP Enterprise

"In clean, concise language—which is rare these days—Harvard grad and successful entrepreneur Jed Yueh explains the concepts of idea, build, and scale as the framework for putting ideas into business models that work. He uses his deep IT business knowledge as a whiteboard for teaching us that we can't sit and be complacent about our businesses—we have to constantly be on the lookout for new efficiencies, new ideas, and new ways to connect with our customers, employees, and partners. Yueh also shows us how to collaborate in order to innovate. There is so much more in this book from which we can all learn."

—CHRIS PREIMESBERGER, Editor, eWEEK.com

"Jed's launched billion-dollar software products and built two successful companies. *Disrupt or Die* takes you inside the mind of a product CEO, perhaps the most valuable real estate in the global economy."

—JEB MILLER, General Partner, Icon Ventures

"As digital disruption is becoming a certainty for virtually every business, perpetuating current modes of thinking, planning, and execution can guarantee extinction. This book provides a breathtaking and sweeping perspective that shows how history and business disruption may not repeat itself, but it often rhymes. Yueh creates useful mental models of what has created the business winners and losers thus far in the emerging digital age, and provides insights and practical strategies and tactics that every business leader should be aware of."

—GENE KIM, Best-Selling Coauthor of *The Phoenix Project* and
The DevOps Handbook

"The most compelling book I've ever read on technology disruption."

—CHRIS LAPING, Best-Selling Author, *People Before Things*

DISRUPT OR DIE

What the World Needs to Learn from Silicon Valley
to Survive the Digital Era

ISBN   978-1-61961-658-5   Hardcover

        978-1-61961-659-2   Paperback

        978-1-61961-660-8   Ebook

LIONCREST
PUBLISHING

DISRUPT
OR DIE

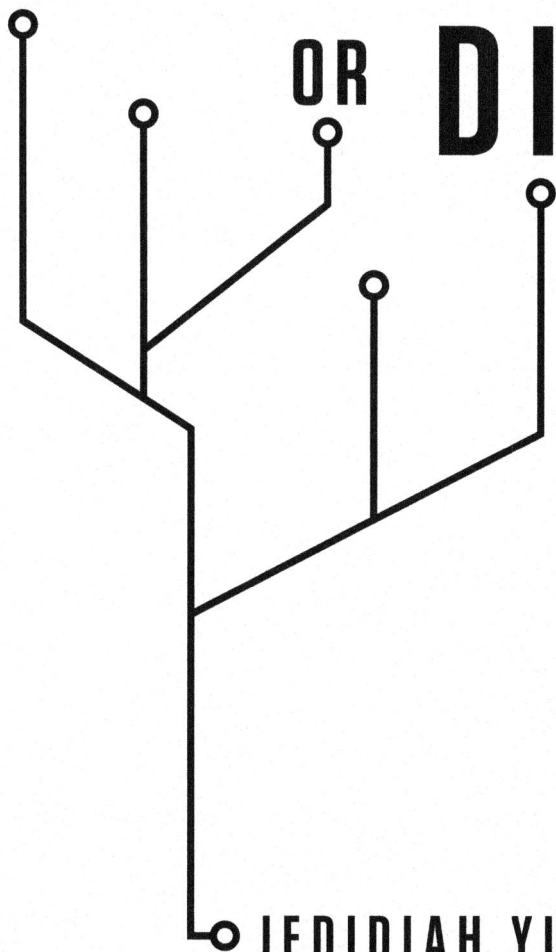

JEDIDIAH YUEH

CONTENTS

INTRODUCTION:
THE ACCIDENTAL ENTREPRENEUR

ALTHOUGH I'VE INVENTED multibillion-dollar software products, I had low expectations for myself growing up. I overheard adults mention that your academic record gets wiped clean when you enter high school, which meant grades in elementary school or junior high were largely pointless. As far as I was concerned, I had a hall pass until I reached high school.

On day one of high school, I finally decided to try. *Selective effort* has been part of my life's ethos ever since.

I apply great effort when I know it will generate great return.

Today, we have reached a point in the development of human history where technology has enabled humans to generate *maximum return for minimum effort*.

Unless you write code or work in technology, you may be thinking that innovation is the domain of the Tech Titans—an intellectual playground for the trained elite.

I've been on a quest to understand digital disruption my entire career. I've accumulated a series of critical frameworks for innovation, by seeking out many of the top entrepreneurs and CEOs of the world's biggest tech companies. I've implemented these frameworks successfully as founding CEO of my own software companies, and I'm sharing them here to help CEOs and executive teams around the world.

Here's my confession as an accidental entrepreneur:

1. I majored in English and psychology.
2. I don't know how to code.
3. I never wanted to be an entrepreneur.[1]

How does a humanities major end up as the founding CEO for not one but two software companies, both deep in the rabbit hole of the modern application and systems stack?

It's a matter of point of view (POV).

Alan Kay, lead researcher at Xerox PARC, birthplace of many of the core innovations that define our lives today, has a motto: "POV is worth 80 IQ points."

This will make more sense in a few minutes.

We've been conditioned all our lives to respect expertise: to listen to doctors, lawyers, and scientists and to accept their recommendations, guidance, and knowledge as a matter of course—to suspend large-scale skepticism so we can benefit from accumulated knowledge and institutional learning.

We're exposed to researchers who uncover the hidden "truths" of success. In *Outliers*, Malcolm Gladwell describes how Bill Gates had early and privileged access to mainframe computer cycles to accumulate the "magic" ten thousand hours required to achieve expertise—long before computer cycles were widely available to other hobbyists and entrepreneurs.

He also spotlights a singular birth year for Tech Titans: 1955,

---

1   I never wanted to be an entrepreneur until I became one.

the year when Bill Gates (Microsoft), Steve Jobs (Apple), Eric Schmidt (Google), and Vinod Khosla and Andreas Bechtolsheim (Sun) were all born—just early enough they could reach the peak of mental acuity and be first to stake their claims in the PC revolution.

And we have the anecdotal evidence. Take the founders of the top seven technology companies in the world—Apple, Alphabet (Google), Amazon, Microsoft, Facebook, Oracle, and Dell—and you'll find odd commonalities. Yes, they are all white males, many from privileged backgrounds, and most of them went to top-four schools by reputation, including Harvard, Stanford, and Princeton. But more curiously, they are all either abandoned, dropouts, or both:[2]

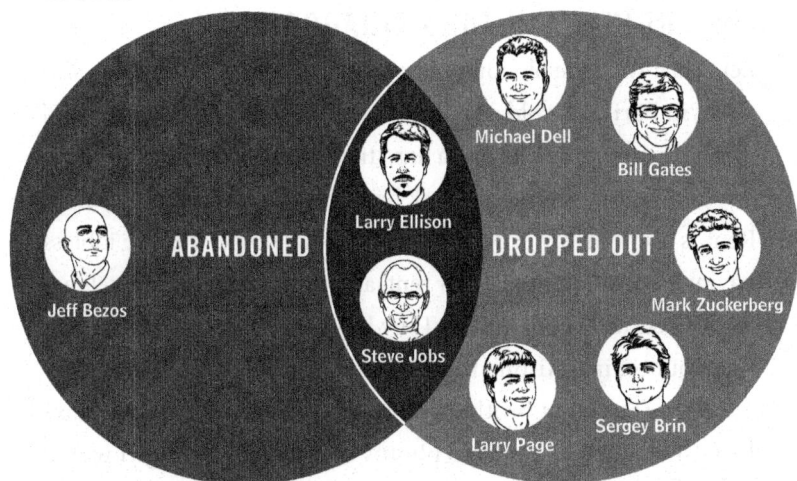

Clearly, it takes unusual opportunity, a tortured psychological past, grueling hours of apprenticeship, a vintage birth year, and an early sense of greater purpose to reach technological success.

---

2   Jeff Bezos was abandoned by his birth father, who didn't know his son had gone on to become a billionaire, until tracked down by a biographer. Larry Page and Sergey Brin dropped out of Stanford's PhD program in computer science.

Or does it?

In my case, I never wanted to be an entrepreneur until I became one. I never accumulated ten thousand hours of experience before I invented my first multibillion-dollar software product (less than five hundred hours). My parents kept me around (for better or worse). And, unfortunately, I graduated from college. I had all the makings of a technology tragedy![3]

You're probably discounting my individual experience, ironically, as an outlier. So, let's consider the founding product insight—the defining moment and critical germ for future success—for some of the most powerful technology companies today.

THE ORDINARY IN THE EXTRAORDINARY

Let's start with the obvious examples. Two men are standing on a street in Paris. It's cold and it's snowing. They've been eating and drinking, and they're having a hard time hailing a cab. Uber is born.

Two friends from New York have just moved to San Francisco. Rent is abominably expensive and getting worse. They're jobless, having a hard time paying for rent, and they notice local hotels are all booked for a conference. They buy a couple airbeds and rent them out online. Airbnb is born.

Two fraternity brothers at Stanford are talking. One says he wishes the questionable photos he's sending to a girl would automatically disappear. The second gets really animated. Snap (formerly Snapchat) is born.

That's over $100 billion in combined market valuation in 2017. You're probably still not convinced.

Let's look at the less obvious examples. A sophomore in college

---

3   Time will tell if 1974 turns out to be a vintage birth year. It's unlikely.

is asked to help code a social networking site exclusive to students at the college. For undergrads, the college publishes a thin, burgundy-colored physical book called the Facebook. He decides to build his own site instead. Facebook is born.

In 2004, Mark Zuckerberg shared with the *Harvard Crimson* that "I do stuff like this all the time. The Facebook literally took me a week to make." He continued, saying, "Half the things I do I don't release." He later added, "If I hadn't launched it that day, I was about to just can it and go on to the next thing I was about to do."

When we look at the scale and complexity of Facebook today, it clouds our memory of where it began, creating a sense of awe and the cognitive illusion of unattainability.

Here's another one. In the world of academia, published papers are often judged by their citations, how often they are cited, and the importance of each citation. Two PhD students decided to apply that concept to counting and weighing the value of links on websites (instead of citations)—an automated way to rank search results. Google is born.

Most of the world thinks that the fantastic innovations coming out of Silicon Valley are just short of magic. But if you look at them from the right *point of view*, they start looking *ordinary*.

The big truth of the technology world we live in today is that the origins are often mundane and achievable—especially for software apps, where maximum leverage is continuing to build.

What about all the engineers you need to hire? All the computer systems you need to manage? All the software you need to write to support millions or billions of users? All the countless decisions in product and company building you need to make?

Today you can buy limitless infrastructure from Amazon Web Services. You can use software that manages and scales across hundreds of thousands of servers for free with Kubernetes, open sourced by Google. You can launch on multiple platforms that give you instant reach to billions of consumers, including iOS, Android, and Facebook. You can hire a team of star developers on Gigster in minutes.

And this book will provide you with the frameworks to make the decisions that come later. Don't be dispirited by the magnitude of complexity ahead. We need to make only one decision at a time. The right decisions eliminate huge branches of wasted work and countless decisions to repair the damage.

We live and work beneath an illusory Innovation Glass Ceiling,[4] near the start of what may be the greatest gold rush human history will ever see.

The purpose of this book is to shatter the illusion.

I'm not saying anyone can do it. It takes brains, guts, and determination to succeed. But it is far more accessible than people think. And it all depends on your point of view.

ABOUT THIS BOOK

This book is organized into three parts. Many of the concepts covered briefly here will come into full clarity in subsequent chapters.

In "The Idea," we start with why successful companies today find it nearly impossible to innovate. We discover what we can learn from evolution, and we identify and exploit opportunities by finding Value Seams in fast-changing markets. We flesh out those ideas with the Innovation Triangle and quickly judge ideas worthy or unworthy with a Value Triangle. Then, we enlist frameworks

---

4   Not to be confused with the very real glass ceiling of gender inequality found in Silicon Valley firms.

to help you learn what you need to learn, and we prepare ideas to take root aggressively and resiliently with the secret weapon of the successful entrepreneur—the Disconfirmation Bias. Finally, we categorically identify the patterns of repeatable success in the Tree of Innovation.

In "The Build," we examine the power of vision, delve into the roles and responsibilities of the leader, and determine how to organize your company for success. We resolve the endless debates over the importance of culture versus talent versus strategy, and so forth, with the Digital Food Chain. We cover how and where to hire the right team and how to obviate competition by building value in layers.

In "The Scale," we look at how proven innovation can be quickly turned into what I call an Appzilla, a software application capable of laying waste to a billion-dollar industry or more. We look first at go-to-market strategies, then watch a play about the death of the salesman, and finally descend into the new Marketing Rabbit Hole. We focus on the Magic Metric that drives success and learn how to pick our battlegrounds among the competing Application Platform Ecosystems (APEs) and Application Solar Systems (ASSes). We learn how to eat or be eaten and how to unlock cyclonic effects that can lay waste to industries.

Finally, we consider the implications of technologies such as AI and automation for humankind.

In college, I wrote a paper on Martin Luther, who changed the world by defiantly posting his famous Ninety-Five Theses on the door of the Wittenberg Castle church. In 1517, Luther challenged the central religious authority of the Catholic Church, arguing that humans could reach salvation directly through their own faith, instead of paying indulgences to priests and the pope—shattering a

spiritual glass ceiling and changing the course of history by spark-
ing the Protestant Reformation, which led to a radical group of
Protestant pilgrims settling in America and the eventual rise of
Silicon Valley.

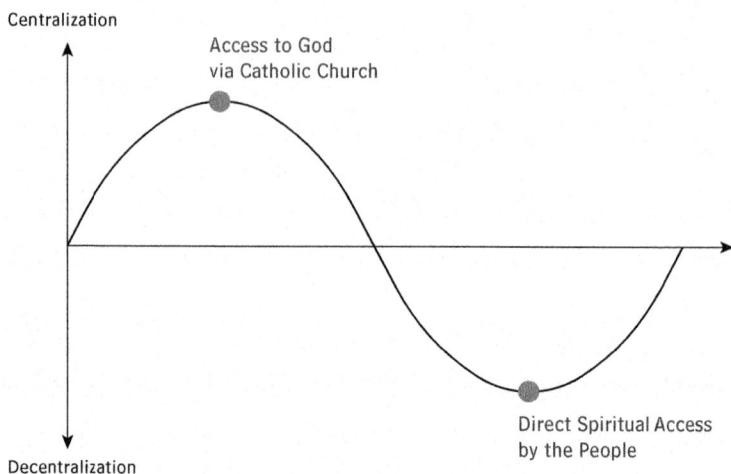

Centralization

Access to God
via Catholic Church

Direct Spiritual Access
by the People

Decentralization

There are no barriers to innovation. No technology priests or
popes to worship—only the illusory conditioning that limits our
minds and actions.

Great innovators gather the cloth of today's technologies until
they pull forward a glimpse of the future. My goal is to pull forward
the innovators on the margin, those trying to disrupt or prevent
disruption, and arm them with the mental models that successful
entrepreneurs use to catalyze their success.

There's never been a better time to apply maximum effort.

PART ONE:
THE IDEA

CHAPTER 1:
I SEE DEAD COMPANIES

N THE MOVIE *The Silence of the Lambs*, FBI agent Clarice Starling turns to Hannibal Lecter for advice on catching a serial killer. "Hannibal the Cannibal" correctly tells Clarice to look where the killings began: "We begin by coveting what we see."

In Silicon Valley, we see startup activities every day: software engineering, hiring and team building, finance, sales and marketing—all the functions of the budding enterprise. As a result, entrepreneurs come to covet the problems they see every day and build solutions for them.

Silicon Valley's insular cycle of "covet and consume" ironically threatens companies across all industries by accelerating the global Innovation Cycle.

When Stewart Butterfield, CEO of gaming startup Tiny Speck, failed to get critical mass with an online game called Glitch, he shut down the former company and looked internally for something to salvage from the wreckage. He found it in their homegrown communications stack, built initially on a text-based communications protocol called Internet Relay Chat (IRC), which they surrounded with developer hacks to add features.

They knew they had found a better way for startups to communicate and collaborate. Instead of returning the remaining venture capital investment, Butterfield relaunched the company around the communications platform, now called Slack.

Slack took off like a rocket ship, reaching $100 million in annual recurring revenue (ARR) three years after launch—faster than any enterprise software company in history. Slack is one of hundreds of companies attacking the daily inhibitors that limit speed, agility, and collaboration in startups.

Inhibitor Feeders like Slack consume the friction and pain points in startups, enabling the broad-scale acceleration of all elements required to turn an idea into a sustainable business.

Developers see and covet development problems every day. As a result, the last few years have seen an explosion in developer-centric tools and platforms, resulting in a major trend—the rise of Application Platform Ecosystems (APEs).

While collaboration tools such as email, Skype, and Google Chat have long existed, Slack focused on a few key elements that enabled its viral adoption, including frictionless user-experience design, creating an open archive for company communications, and enabling developer hacks—a developer platform and ecosystem that has woven Slack's roots into myriad products, tools, and processes. These integrations deepen Slack's value and further entrench their platform into the modern computing ecosystem.

Today, instead of developing platforms and companies for end users, we see developer-oriented versions of products—products designed for software as the end user. These products, such as Mailgun, Stripe, and hundreds of DevOps tools, connect via application programming interfaces (APIs) to create *layered software stacks*—invisible, highly coupled infrastructure that powers many of the fastest growing technology companies today.

The sum of these Inhibitor Feeders ensures that digital disruption will happen faster and easier than ever before. Every company that attacks another friction point in the evolving technology stack adds digital grease to the tracks, accelerating the Innovation Cycle.

Software has a manifest destiny to grow faster, casting an ominous shadow over legacy companies around the world.

DIGITAL ELEPHANTS

A few weeks before Well Fargo's very public accounts scandal, I had dinner with John Stumpf, when he reigned as one of the great CEOs in the company's history. At the time, he oversaw the largest financial services company in the world by market capitalization and had shepherded the company through quarters in excess of $5 billion in net earnings (second only to Apple in quarterly wealth generation).

John is an engaging, charming host, warm and accessible beneath a full head of gray hair. Over drinks, we talked about the threat of FinTech, the hundreds of startup piranha that have emerged to hungrily chew off a share of the $171 billion in annual profits generated by the US banking industry in 2016.

I asked John how important technology and disruption were to his business, and his face turned serious. "Very important." He nodded. "There's almost nothing more important."

I asked him a second question, one that illustrates the need for this book: "How much time per week do you personally spend focusing on technology and innovation?"

Having worked with several companies of the same scale, such as Walmart, Bank of America, and JPMorgan Chase, I had my suspicions.

John inclined his head and lowered his voice to just above a whisper. "Less than you think."

And behold: the Digital Elephant in the room.

Startups know and behave like they have a small chance of survival. While many slow-moving legacy companies know their chances for maintaining their industry positions are quickly deteriorating, they fail to behave like it.

Let's look at the retail industry by the numbers. Over the last decade, Amazon has ravenously consumed much of the market value across the industry and all but closed off the oxygen for growth.

Change in Market Value (2006-2016)

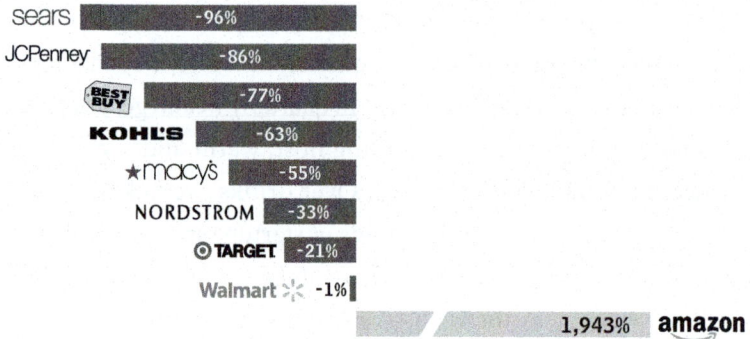

Company	Change
sears	-96%
JCPenney	-86%
BEST BUY	-77%
KOHL'S	-63%
★macy's	-55%
NORDSTROM	-33%
TARGET	-21%
Walmart	-1%
amazon	1,943%

Yet every retailer and consumer packaged goods (CPG) company on the planet *thinks* it has a digital strategy. Retail and CPG giants spend a fortune on information technology, and many of them have invested heavily in websites, apps, and an "omni-channel strategy," where they can sell and market their goods across all available channels, such as mobile devices, web browsers, social media platforms, catalogs, and physical stores.

But these are the lies we tell ourselves.

I've spent the last two decades driving two waves of transformation in enterprise data management. I've spent most of my adult life on airplanes, flying from city to city, meeting with CEOs, COOs, CFOs, and CIOs of the world's largest companies—helping them modernize their infrastructure, so they can better respond to the changing world around them.

Many of them have invited me to look at their innovation centers, think tanks, and labs, where they showcase their best and brightest pursuing the latest in technology.

Yet I've never heard a single great idea presented to me. It's the innovation Kabuki theater—all activity and drama, with no real progress.

In all those years, I've never had a client ask me for critical feedback and collaboration on *their* best ideas (they just want us to support what they think they already know)—despite a track record as a successful serial entrepreneur.

If you have an innovation practice, chances are you're fooling yourself into thinking you're doing the right things—it's a funhouse mirror to hide the reality of a dead company walking.

Innovation programs often focus on named, industry-recognizable challenges, such as the omni-channel strategy.

It's not a strategy, however, if all your competitors are following the same plan. It's unplanned obsolescence. If you're following the herd, you're falling further and further behind the rising digital leaders, and your odds of survival are plummeting.

But what if you could radically reverse those odds?

RISE OF APPZILLA

As we've established, today's apps grow bigger and faster than ever before. We've reached an inflection point where the rate of development for a killer app has accelerated by an order of magnitude over the prior decade—and it will surely accelerate by another order of magnitude over the next decade as well.

Appzillas are the apex predators in any new technology category. They are the killer apps that transform businesses and make their competitors look antiquated overnight. They inhabit the dreams of entrepreneurs and venture capitalists and fuel the nightmares of Luddites and legacy industry chiefs.

Amazon's cloud feeds hundreds of thousands of applications and has already enabled the evolution of Appzillas such as Airbnb—software predators capable of consuming billions in revenue and disrupting long-standing industry kings. All the core infrastructure that went into building giants like Google and Amazon have become commodities, often available for free or as a service by the drink.

Technology has laid a foundation that allows nontechnical, mundane ideas to grow into hugely disruptive monsters.

Last year, I had breakfast with David Castellani, SVP and business information officer of New York Life. David is awake to the threat of disruption. He's a tall, fit executive with a hawk-like stare. He doesn't look in the funhouse mirror, so he knows the real odds, and he candidly shared the challenges of grappling with transformation.

David and many industry executives are victims of their own success. With their command of operations, David said the executive team can simply roll out of bed in the morning, and New York Life will hit its numbers and pay its bonuses. But cultures of complacency and success are their own worst enemies.

How safe is New York Life from Appzillas and their growing tails?

When the iPhone emerged as a new, pristine application ecosystem, few could have predicted the long tail of creation and destruction that would tear across industries and the world. Technologies, like living organisms, interact in myriad ways, creating highly interconnected food chains that can enable surprising consequences in far-flung industries.

We're not talking about how Apple, the pioneer of the PC, created a computing device with an embedded camera that put Kodak out of business. Or how the iPhone made the array of mobile phones and merged-PDA devices such as the BlackBerry look antiquated overnight. Those events are too obvious.

We're talking about subtler compound effects, such as the domino chain of location-mapping data sources (e.g., Google Maps) combined with foundational data technologies such as GPS in phones. The match gave rise to apps such as Uber, which first rampaged through the taxi industry and has set its eyes on an even more prized, emerging habitat—autonomous vehicles.

Looking further down the line, we can see this Appzilla's tail continuing to lengthen. As autonomous vehicles emerge (we've seen them driving of their own accord up and down 280 and 101 in Silicon Valley for years), the data in the vehicles provide a disproportionate advantage to those who consolidate, control, and manufacture these fleets to better calculate … *insurance premiums.*

The data collected from self-driving cars can make automobile insurers look as blind as the statue of justice to what they really need to know about their insured drivers. According to a Morgan Stanley report, up to 80 percent of the revenue of some of the world's largest insurers may be in jeopardy due to potential disruption by autonomous vehicle technology providers.

Even worse, insurers often use automobile insurance as a loss leader to enable upsell and cross-sell of other insurance products, such as home and life insurance. Technology companies, once they get a foothold, could follow that path, spreading into other insurance categories.

When technology companies have eaten their share of their initial markets, they will hunger for new sources of growth, and the insurance industry is a sweet, rich pie.

The tail doesn't stop there.

Insurance companies, and the vast sums of capital they maintain to safeguard against major disasters, play a critical role in global banking and investments. If technology companies consume those capital streams, it's nearly certain they will disproportionately invest their capital in further innovation, creating a self-perpetuating Cyclone of transformation.

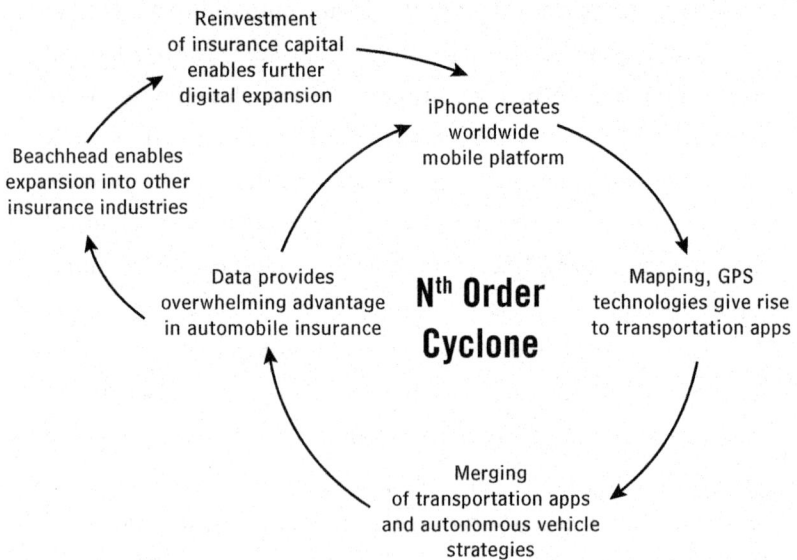

Reinvestment of insurance capital enables further digital expansion

iPhone creates worldwide mobile platform

Beachhead enables expansion into other insurance industries

Data provides overwhelming advantage in automobile insurance

Nth Order Cyclone

Mapping, GPS technologies give rise to transportation apps

Merging of transportation apps and autonomous vehicle strategies

Software enables the wholesale destruction of industry eco-systems and the emergence of new evolutionary dynamics. It's the second-, fifth-, and nth-order effects of cumulative innovation that will whiplash across today's complacent industry kings.

And yet, the world behaves almost as if in denial.

Yes, we all hear stories of Silicon Valley, where geeks go to become gods. But in the rest of the world, in industries that have been built over decades of competition with roots reaching back to the Industrial Revolution, the threat of digital revolution is often muted, muffled by layers of management, and drowned by the siren song of quarterly revenue achievement.

It's time to wake up.

CHAPTER 2:

THINKING BIG AND SMALL

O N MY FIRST day of college, I followed orientation instructions that led me downstairs into the basement of the science center. I found myself standing in a dimly lit room with rows of computers and big, clunky monitors that cast a faint glow on attentive faces. The instructions told me how to log in to one of the unoccupied computers and set up a username, which generated my first email address: jedidiah.yueh@harvard.edu.

It was 1992. I had never heard of an email address and didn't know what to do with one. What was with the "@" sign anyway? I looked around to see if anyone could fill me in, but the other students sat in a catatonic state, eyes glued to their monitors.

I didn't know it at the time, but the first web browser had just been released and the Internet had mushroomed into a towering digital cloud, sweeping quickly across the world. Silicon Valley was powering ahead, and I was unknowingly falling behind.

Why did I need an email address? Who was I going to email?

I frowned at the blinking monitor, a little itch in the back of my mind that I was missing something important.[5] A moment later, I broke the spell, stood up, and left to find a real, physical mailbox.

It would take me another seven years, but I would eventually be sucked into the rabbit hole of the Internet.

THINKING BIG

Once you paid for tuition, Harvard didn't charge you by the number of courses you took, so instead of the standard four courses, I often took five or six, while working up to three part-time jobs to help pay for college.[6]

I pursued courses that reframed the world around me: plate tectonics, evolutionary biology, quantum mechanics, neuroscience, Freudian psychology, economics, and the development and underdevelopment of nations.

As I learned concepts that helped me reinterpret the world, I learned that human history itself is an iterative story of reinterpreting the world, a series of successive, overlapping cycles.

We began with primitive stories, which gave way to legends, which gave way to mythology, which gave way to religions, which gave rise to science, which has ultimately led to modern technology.

Stories   Legends   Mythology   Religion   Science   Technology

---

5   My entire future, it turns out.
6   Even with three jobs and tens of thousands of dollars in scholarships, I still ended up with a pile of debt!

Our universe and the technology world inside it are also governed by overlapping cycles, specifically cycles of centralization and decentralization.

We started with the centralized origins of the universe, followed by the big bang that scattered substance across the cosmos. Our solar system began with a centralizing gravitational mass that triggered an explosion—a continuous nuclear fusion reactor. Land emerged on the planet in a single, concentrated continent called Pangaea, only to decentralize into smaller continents and islands over time. Human life emerged in a single location in Africa, dispersed across the world, and then recentralized in great cities and nations.

Our technology world is no different. It began with centralized mainframe computing, which broke apart with the rise of the PC. Commodity servers, PCs, and later mobile devices proliferated before the rise of cloud computing, a new wave of centralization. With the Internet of things (IoT) seeding CPUs into everything and everywhere, another wave of decentralization has emerged.

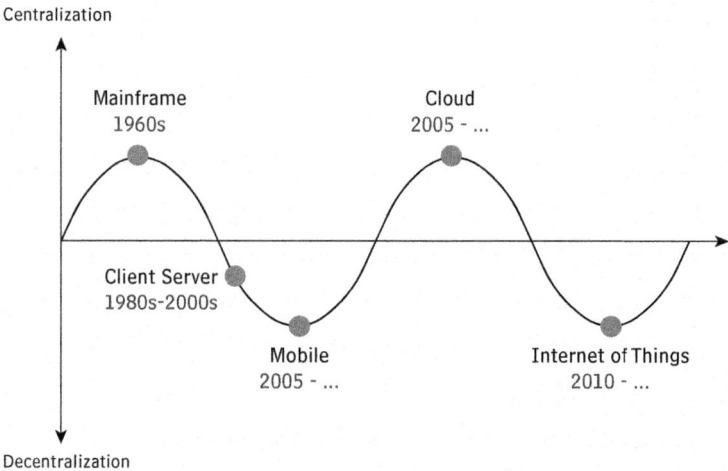

But the cycle times in the digital era are compressing, and our future will be written by ever faster cycles of centralization and decentralization.

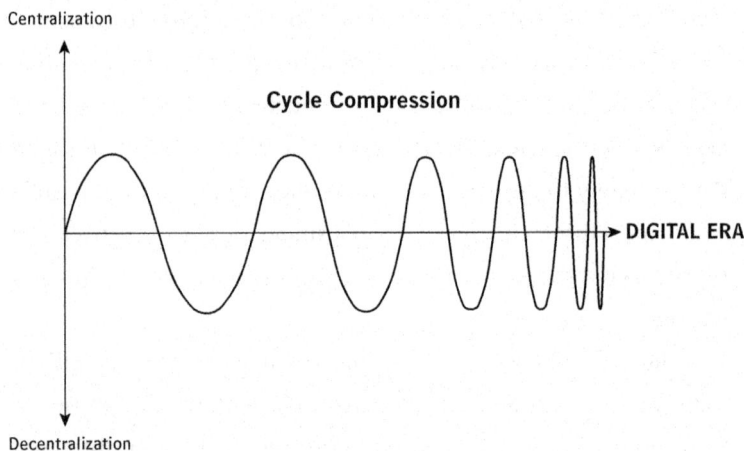

Centralization

Cycle Compression

DIGITAL ERA

Decentralization

The courses I took in college taught me the importance of thinking big, of keeping an open mind to a point of view (POV) that could change what you believe about everything.

THE DIGITAL RABBIT HOLE

In college, I thought I would end up in academia as an English professor and write books on the side. At least I got half of it right.

My white rabbit was a summer consulting internship for a data storage company building network-attached optical jukeboxes— like a musical jukebox but for enterprise data. My first job was to model their widget factory in Excel.[7]

---

7   Spreadsheets, finance, and a deep understanding of unit economics are key tools for entrepreneurs to master.

Given my natural inclination to think big, I started by researching the industry. At the time, the fundamental media economics of the data storage industry was in flux. Enterprises used expensive disk storage for their most valuable data and inexpensive tape storage for less critical data.

The startup I worked for wanted to be the third, just-right bed that Goldilocks selected. Optical disks, such as CD-Rs and CD-RWs, were less expensive than disk but faster in access speeds than tape (also more expensive than tape and slower than disk).

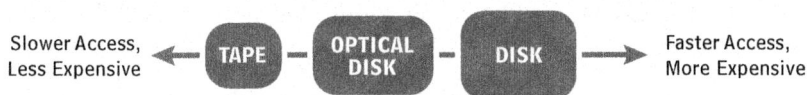

Slower Access, Less Expensive ← TAPE – OPTICAL DISK – DISK → Faster Access, More Expensive

With a little research, you could see that the cost of disk storage was plummeting versus tape and optical disk over time—a macrotrend that would soon upend the data storage industry and the value thesis for the jukebox company.

I decided the sensible course was to challenge the CEO. How would the company make its way out of a narrowing alleyway?

The CEO couldn't answer the question, so he called a meeting of the heads of state, including the head of hardware engineering, head of software engineering, project management, and so on. They couldn't answer my questions either.

In the end, they offered me a bigger job, but I knew I couldn't solve an unsolvable problem. While I eventually left the company, I had discovered something important that would change my life: a Value Seam.

VALUE SEAMS

Value Seams are the obvious gaping holes in the world. Despite their size, they can be hard to find. They may not look valuable until you find them, but once you find one, you can't let it go.

Your POV is changed forever.

As detailed in the court documents about the founding dispute at Snap, Evan Spiegel reportedly started jumping around after his fraternity brother shared the idea of automatically disappearing incriminating photos (also known as "d*&k pics"). Evan blurted out something to the effect of, "That's a million-dollar idea!"

He was incredibly wrong about that. It was a *multibillion-dollar* idea.

While Spiegel made the clear jump to product (it was straightforward at the time to build a photo-sharing app that deletes pictures), I had a Value Seam but didn't know how to take advantage of it.

Instead, I continued to explore the seam. I quickly discovered that the right industry to target was a sector of the data storage industry—the $4 billion hardware and software market for tape backup and recovery.

Companies backed up the same data over and over again each week for all their systems. After a few weeks, they would ship older tapes by truck to archive facilities reminiscent of the last scene out of *Raiders of the Lost Ark*.

I also learned the backup industry had terrible success rates. Backups failed 20 percent of the time, and restores failed 30 percent of the time. Companies paid for systems, software, tapes, tape transportation, and archiving, only to have it fail when they needed it most.

It was a terrible industry. It was a glorious opportunity.

In addition, I knew consumer domains were undergoing a parallel transformation. MP3 players had proliferated like bunny rabbits, shifting music from tapes to disk, while improving user experience. And TiVo had just launched, shifting VHS tapes to disk, with an even better increase in user experience.

It was a Value Seam begging to be filled.

If you're an innovator in a large enterprise, you have an incredible advantage in finding Value Seams. You have deep knowledge of how your industry works and how your company differentiates. You have access to insider data. You can learn every step along major use cases by speaking with customers.

But how do you go from a big-picture Value Seam to inventing the right product?

THINKING SMALL

I still remember the day the idea struck me—it was a sunny day, and I was sitting at a Diedrich Coffee in Irvine, California.

The rest of it was art imitating life. In the HBO show *Silicon Valley*, the awkward, skinny protagonist invents a superior algorithm for compressing data. He then launches the company, raises money from VCs, and has to decide whether to build a software platform or a hardware appliance they can sell to enterprises.

We did the same things two decades earlier, and I doubt the directors and writers of the show even know anything about Avamar.

Once I understood the basic functioning of the systems that underpin data storage—file systems, volume managers, RAID, and so forth—I realized there was no need to back up the same data over and over again.

Enterprise backup to tape wasn't like audiocassettes and VHS tapes, which stored *different* songs, TV shows, and movies.

Enterprises took full backups of the *same data* every week. In addition, a great deal of it was the same data *across multiple different systems* (e.g., the same Windows operating system files across hundreds of servers and the same PowerPoint files sent to hundreds of email inboxes).

Thinking Small is the act of product invention. It's taking everything you know about a Value Seam and distilling it into a product that gives you power over that Value Seam. It's the reimagining of what's possible in user experience.

The moment of innovation is the lightning leap between big and small.

The backup industry was like that terrible scene from *The Matrix Reloaded* where hundreds of duplicate Agent Smiths appear at every turn.

By eliminating duplicate data across time and systems (killing Agent Smith), we had a technical invention that could accelerate the economic superiority of disk versus tape (and optical disk), pulling the future forward by more than a decade and creating a lever arm we could use to displace a multibillion-dollar industry.

And that is what actually happened.

THINKING BIG AND SMALL

In *Thinking, Fast and Slow*, Daniel Kahneman, winner of the Nobel Prize in economics, describes our two modes of thinking. We have a fast, intuitive system that is gullible and jumps to conclusions. We also have a slow, rational system that is deliberate, systematic, and lazy.

Unfortunately, the fast, gullible system secretly hijacks the rational system on a regular basis, resulting in all kinds of unintended errors and biases.

No wonder the world is as crazy as it is today.

This dialectic between our two systems of thinking is the quirky essence of human nature. And it's the dialectic of Thinking Big and Small that is the essence of innovation.

Now, I'm sure other entrepreneurs describe their experiences differently. And what works for me might not work for you. After all, the principles behind Eric Ries's "Lean Startup Method" and Steve Blank's iterative "Customer Development" practices didn't apply to me.

Steve Blank is a Silicon Valley institution. His website is a time machine back to the 1990s. A student of his course at Stanford, Eric Ries, authored *The Lean Startup*, based on Blank's advocacy of a hypothesis-driven approach called Customer Development, where entrepreneurs test their hypotheses about their products and business models with iterative customer reviews. Then they develop a minimum viable product (MVP) for further testing.

I didn't know about *The Lean Startup* when I started and later sold my first software company. And I ignored all the principles of Customer Development at Delphix. I simply wrote up all the requirements, we developed the products, and we started selling them—just by Thinking Big and Small.

If you must iterate, by all means iterate. The only cost of iterative customer reviews is the opportunity cost of time and effort.

And the world is filled with successes that violate lean principles, of course.

iPods and iPhones shipped in highly functional form, hardly MVPs. Teslas shipped with high fit and finish, or they would have been dead on the showroom floor. And if Mark Zuckerberg had taken the time to review his initial ideas for the Facebook platform with a structured series of customer reviews (instead of coding it up in a week), the Winklevoss twins might now be sitting atop one of the five biggest companies in the world.[8]

And the data shows that startups still die at an alarming rate, whether they're run lean or not.

The fastest, cheapest form of failure is the iterative success and failure of ideas in the process of Thinking Big and Small—in the mind of the innovator. What survives the well-trained mind just might grow up into an Appzilla.

---

8   That was meant to be facetious, because I doubt they would have made the same series of decisions that resulted in the long-term success of Facebook.

CHAPTER 3:

THE INNOVATION TRIANGLE

Two roads diverged in a digital wood, and
luckily, I could travel both and be one traveler.

—*A little more Robert Frost than me*

MET MARC ANDREESSEN and Ben Horowitz, who run the well-known VC firm Andreessen Horowitz (A16Z) shortly after we closed a financing round at Delphix, my second software company. Marc cofounded Netscape, which put the power of the Internet at the fingertips of the entire world, and Ben founded Opsware, which sold to HP for $1.6 billion.

Marc is a tall, imposing figure with an elevated head that accentuates his commanding intellect, and Ben has the eyes of a digital war veteran mixed with an easy, jovial conversational style.

If there's one great shortcut to digital success, it's to find successful founders and early CEOs who are deeply vested in your mission and have the time to help.

In our meeting, we had a high-throttle conversation where we discussed the technology industry at large, where Delphix would carve out its market, and Marc and Ben's philosophy on investments.

In the high-tech world, we often order the way we think based on technology concepts.

This was a high-bandwidth conversation, with an incredible amount of information passed back and forth on multiple levels (technology, business, emotional maturity, etc.). All that high-bandwidth data was processed at high clock-speeds (referring to CPU speed), with ideas reviewed, discarded, and accepted in minutes.

You can feel the difference as easily as you can feel the strength of a handshake. It's like connecting via dial-up on an x86 PC from 1999 versus a fiber connection on a modern MacBook. In fact, when I interview people, I rate them on a 1 to 10 scale on clock-speed and bandwidth.

We already had two marquee firms as anchor investors in Delphix—Greylock Partners and Lightspeed Venture Partners—so we didn't have a chance to work closely with Marc and Ben.[9]

PRODUCT-MARKET FIT

Luckily, Marc and Ben are both prolific writers. In addition to coining the ethos for Silicon Valley, "software is eating the world," Marc wrote a post, titled "The Only Thing That Matters," about a concept used liberally in startups: Product-Market Fit (PMF).

In the article, Marc refers to a conversation with Andy Rachleff, a Benchmark Capital cofounder. I met Andy when Benchmark invested in my first software company, Avamar.

Marc relayed Andy's "Law of Startup Success," which says:

The #1 company-killer is lack of market.
- When a great team meets a lousy market, market wins.
- When a lousy team meets a great market, market wins.

---

9   We ended up making a little room for A16Z to invest in Delphix.

- When a great team meets a great market, something special happens.

You can obviously screw up a great market—and that has been done, and not infrequently—but assuming the team is baseline competent and the product is fundamentally acceptable, a great market tends to equal success and a poor market tends to equal failure. Market matters most.

Further, Andy's "Corollary of Startup Success" states:

The only thing that matters is getting to product/market fit.

The life of any startup can be divided into two parts: before product/market fit (call this "BPMF") and after product/market fit ("APMF").

When you are BPMF, focus obsessively on getting to product/market fit.

Do whatever is required ... including changing out people, rewriting your product, moving into a different market, telling customers no when you don't want to, telling customers yes when you don't want to, raising that fourth round of highly dilutive venture capital—whatever is required.

Anyone who's worked for me will tell you that I regularly refer to PMF, which I'd like to explain before I explain how it's broken.

WHAT'S MISSING IN PRODUCT-MARKET FIT

Marc Benioff came up with the idea for Salesforce.com (SFDC), a company with a $65 billion market cap in 2017, in a dream. I met him briefly at a conference. His appearance is starkly at odds with a person who takes spiritual treks to see gurus in India. It's hard to say, but it's at least possible that he's capable of Thinking Big and Small in his dreams. In any case, SFDC illustrates what's missing in PMF.

Siebel Systems established salesforce automation (SFA) as a major enterprise application long before Marc started SFDC. SFA is basically a glorified spreadsheet to track all the opportunities for salespeople in a company.

SFDC, especially at the outset, didn't require any product innovation of significance.[10] The product had already been invented. Marc's great innovation was a simple matter of addition: existing product + newish business model + bottom-up go-to-market (GTM) strategy.

Marc saw an enormous Value Seam in an enormous market. At its peak, Siebel sold nearly $2 billion a year with a market cap of $30 billion. Fort Knox, however, sat atop a rickety house of cards. Customers had to pay as much as $1.8 million in first-year costs to get the software deployed in-house, and then up to 65 percent of the licenses became shelfware—never deployed or used.

Prior to SFDC, small technology companies already sold and marketed software over the Internet as application service providers (ASPs), but they mistimed the market and the maturity of networks, paddling out well before the wave began to crest.

Instead of selling software on-premises, Marc sold software-as-a-service (SaaS) over the Internet: multitenant software hosted on his systems and sold by the drink in a subscription model.

He combined the newish business model with a different GTM strategy. Instead of using high-paid direct software salespeople to

---

10 Requirements such as multitenancy, scalability of a single application, and so forth are commonplace requirements in software. They require work and intelligent execution, but they do not qualify as significant innovation.

attack the world's biggest accounts, he initially offered freemium trials, targeting startups and small businesses, which converted to paid customers via telesales.

	SIEBEL	EARLY SALESFORCE
PRODUCT	SFA, CRM Software	SFA, CRM Software, but Hosted, Multitenant
BUSINESS MODEL	On-Premises Software License Sales and Services	SaaS
GTM	Direct Sales to Large Companies	Freemium + Telesales to Small and Medium-Sized Businesses (SMBs), Startups

The product alone would not have yielded the market. It was a matter of product + business model + GTM success, which forms the Innovation Triangle.

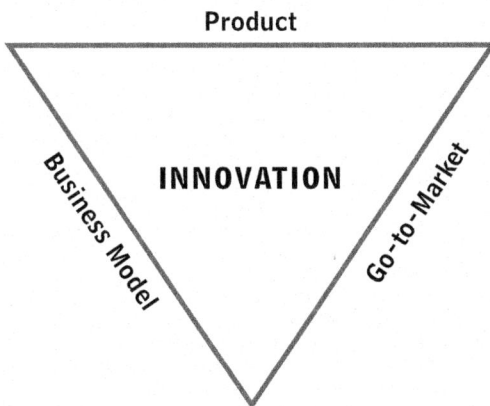

For Salesforce.com, their early Innovation Triangle looked like this:

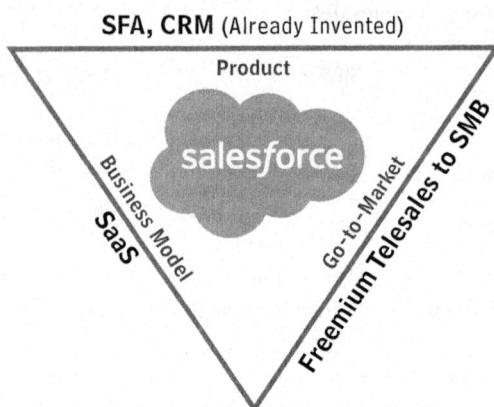

SFA, CRM (Already Invented)
Product

salesforce

Business Model
SaaS

Go-to-Market
Freemium Telesales to SMB

One of the most important points in this book is that innovators need to build business models and GTM strategies *into* the development of their products, when and where they can.

Slack, for instance, ensured that their product was lightweight and easily accessible over the Internet, so they could enable free, viral adoption as their GTM strategy.

I learned the important nuances of this lesson the hard way, which is a story for later. The question for now is: how valuable is your idea?

CHAPTER 4:
THE VALUE TRIANGLE

MET ANDREAS BECHTOLSHEIM in a basement when he was selling used technology equipment.[11] Andy is a Silicon Valley legend, and one of the original founders of Sun. He is ridiculously hands-on, humble, and frugal despite his success. He has a gentle soul, balanced by the world's most advanced mind in networking technology, and he speaks with a faint German accent. As a founder and angel investor, he's accumulated over $5 billion across several companies.

He recently took his latest "startup" public: Arista Networks ($11.3 billion market cap in 2017). He cofounded Arista with his longtime technology partner, David Cheriton. David's another Silicon Valley legend, and together, they have invested in companies such as VMware and my software company, Delphix.

Andy told me a story that shaped how I think about "What Is Most Important When" (WIMIW) in the life of a startup.

---

11 We subleased a basement-level office from Arista when we expanded our offices at Delphix and moved to Menlo Park. It didn't hurt that the office was a five-minute walk from my house.

THE ULTIMATE VALUE SEAM

David called Andy one day and asked him to come over. At the time, David was one of the leading professors of computer science at Stanford, and two graduate students wanted to pitch them their idea.

Huddled around a table, the gangly students opened a laptop. In the center of a white screen sat a low, simple rectangle. Beneath it sat two buttons. One said, "Search." The other said, "I'm Feeling Lucky."

The logo read: "Google."

The two students answered a few questions. How many sites had they indexed? At what speed? What volume of searches were they seeing? How many servers and how much storage had they consumed? How would they monetize the solution? How much did they think they could charge for online micro-advertisements?

Andy did a little math in his head. He quickly concluded: this business will never run out of money. He admits he had no idea how quickly and how large this Appzilla's monetary tail would scale, but he knew it would succeed.

This is what Google's first Innovation Triangle looked like:

The only significant elements left to invent were online auctions and AdWords. Otherwise, they had the core innovation that still powers the majority of the revenue for the second-largest company on the planet ($680 billion market cap in 2017).

They had ripped open a seam in the most important, fastest growing market in the world: the Internet. Cash would rain unabated from that seam in one of the biggest torrential downpours in the history of capitalism.

THE VALUE TRIANGLE

Andy and David each wrote a check on the spot for $100,000, made out to Google Inc. Larry Page and Sergey Brin walked out of David's home wondering how they would cash a check made out to a company that did not yet exist. It was time to incorporate Google Inc. (now owned by its parent company called Alphabet).

Andy has made more than a billion on his own ideas. He made far more on his investment in Google, which he considers the best decision in his entire life.

But most innovations and opportunities are not quite as obvious. How can you quickly assess the potential value of a technology company or idea, so you can pursue or pass?

Here are the three sides to the Value Triangle, a simple framework for determining pursue or pass: Market, Value Differential, and Time to Value (TTV).

Each side of the framework has an acceptance range. If you're out of the range on any side, pass. For Market, you want a size between $100 million to $100 billion+ in total addressable market (TAM). You can increase or decrease the lower end of the range depending on the scale of your company's revenues, the size of your VC fund, or your personal ambition.

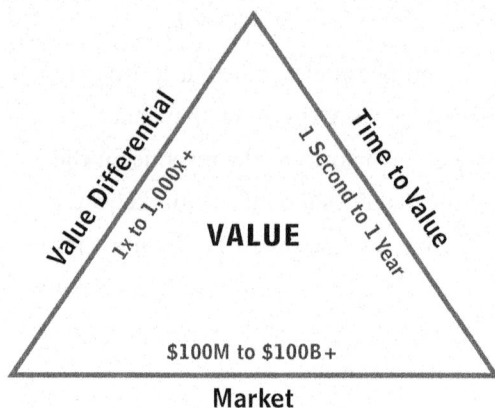

Value Differential
1x to 1,000x+

Time to Value
1 Second to 1 Year

VALUE

$100M to $100B+

Market

If you're the chief of a large legacy company with $10 billion in revenue, the potential market size should be at least 20 percent or $2 billion.

For Value Differential, you're looking at the value you add in the market compared to the best alternative or competitor—your unique value proposition. There may be several factors you might consider here, such as speed, quality, cost, and size.

Pick one, two, or three factors that are most important to winning your market. Value Differential ranges from 1x to 1,000x (100 percent to 100,000 percent improvement). If you count your benefits in percentages, such as 1 percent, 10 percent, or 50 percent, your Value Differential is too low in the world of technology, where 100x and 1,000x benefits exist.[12] Small percentage benefits can win in legacy markets, but they're not worth pursuing in the digital era.

TTV makes up the last side of the triangle and ranges from one second to one year. If your product takes longer than one year for value to be proven, pass.

Now, let's take a look at Google's Value Triangle.

---

12 If you provide net new functionality, such as Snap's disappearing pictures, your advantage in that area is effectively infinite or >1,000x.

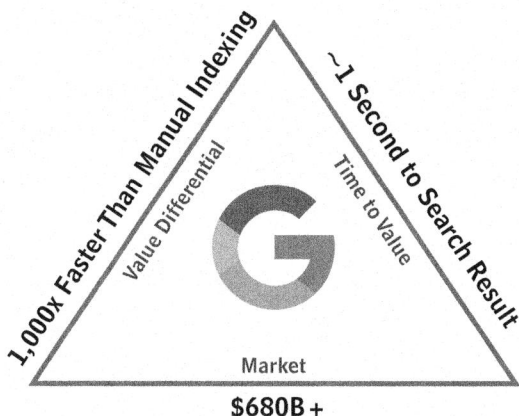

Value Differential

1,000x Faster Than Manual Indexing

~1 Second to Search Result

Time to Value

Market

$680B +

At the time, Yahoo was the eight-thousand-pound Appzilla in the market. Google's algorithmic Page-Rank search had an enormous advantage over Yahoo's manual categorization, probably greater than 1,000x in speed, which provided superior search results compared to Yahoo and other now-defunct search engines.

An important and less understood advantage, however, is Google's incredible TTV. You can type and get a search result in as little as a second if you think and type quickly, a ridiculously fast TTV for users.

Over the years, Google has maintained the simplicity and elegance of their original, unassuming rectangle on a white web page. Yahoo and the other casualties of the market cluttered their pages with headlines, content, banner advertisements, and flashing neon signs that competed with their search offerings—creating cognitive load or a small mental hurdle for users.

Google prioritized every microsecond advantage they had in TTV, ensuring that users had the single best experience on their site when it came to searching the Internet.[13]

---

13   In 2017, Google announced it would finally add a content feed to its search home page, after establishing itself as a near monopoly in search.

Stepping down from Google's Mount Olympus, we can take a look at the Delphix Value Triangle:

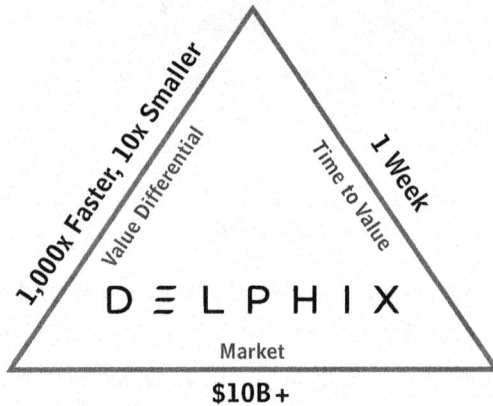

If you want to ship apps fast that work on day one, you need to test apps fast.

When it comes to provisioning data into app environments for testing, Delphix turns months into minutes, a 1,000x advantage over existing alternatives. Our data fuels environments for app testing, running AI algorithms, and moving applications to or between clouds such as Amazon Web Services and Microsoft Azure. We also reduce data storage costs by 10x, eliminating duplicate data across environments by sharing the underlying data blocks. Our software can be installed in hours on-premises or in minutes in the cloud, and customers see benefits in as little as a week.

Our Value Triangle is why the world's biggest brands—Apple, Facebook, JPMorgan, Nike, Walmart, HP, Dell, and more—use our software to pump data into the projects that fuel their businesses.

THE SEPARATION OF USERS AND BUYERS

Thomas Jefferson spoke of the separation of church and state in the framing of the First Amendment to the Constitution of the United States, ensuring one of the fundamental pillars of life in America today.

In the digital era, one of the founding keys to success lies in the Separation of Users and Buyers.

Google's simple home page is just the tip of the iceberg when it comes to their overall advantage in TTV. Compared to other sites and products in other industries, they have the overwhelming advantage that their users do not need to buy their search product at all, forever.

Their users pay $0. And they get the most comprehensive, fastest access to all the data in the world.

Only advertisers, their buyers, have to pay. As a result, Google was able to focus first on value creation for users and then later on scaling their advertising business model.

Other technology giants such as Facebook also built large bases of value independent of their business models and GTM execution, one of the key reasons their valuations preceded their revenues by such incredible amounts.

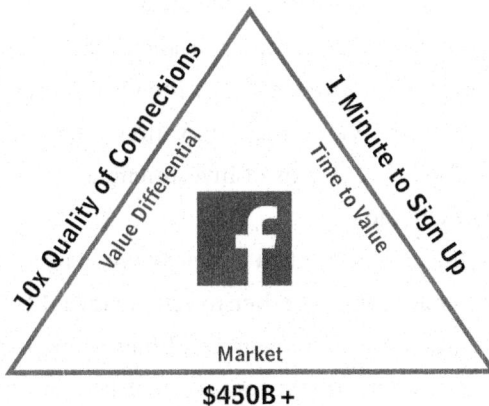

10x Quality of Connections

Value Differential

1 Minute to Sign Up

Time to Value

Market

$450B +

Separation of Users and Buyers isn't a new concept. A long time ago, in a galaxy far, far away, innovative radio stations built their initial audiences by playing music free of advertising. After securing their listening bases, they would slowly add in advertising to monetize the value they had built.

Even enterprise software companies such as Slack and Salesforce.com have employed this strategy, one of the key reasons they grew usage and revenue so quickly over time.

The Innovation Triangle and the Value Triangle are simple frameworks that help innovators understand the core of their innovation and judge its potential value. Once you understand what's most important about the idea and opportunity, you can weigh it against the usual suspects: risk, time, effort, and capital required for execution.

ONE LAST TRIANGLE

Legacy, established companies work within an existing ownership structure, so they do not need to worry as much about an ownership strategy. Unfortunately, they also have less ownership and upside to provide innovators, which is why so many of these innovators leave to start their own businesses.

For entrepreneurs, there's one last triangle that matters, which I will cover briefly. The three sides of the Ownership Triangle, which nests inside the Value and Innovation Triangles, include the Capitalization Table, Terms of Investment, and composition of the Board of Directors.

As you build your idea into a business, you'll need to decide on initial ownership and whether to take external funding. If you decide to pursue the VC route, as I have done in the past, the terms of investment will set control, board composition, and

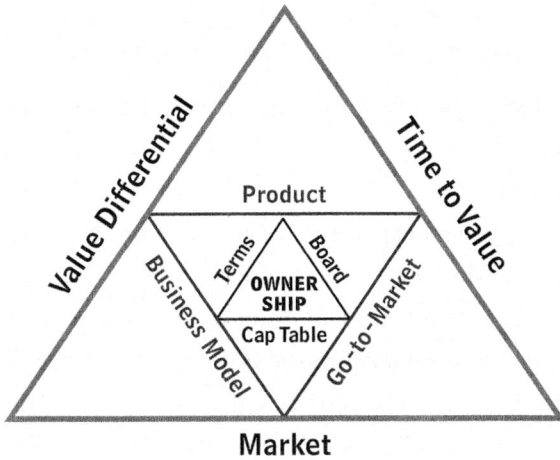

initial capitalization of the company (ownership of shares of the company).

VCs negotiate terms of investment by looking several moves ahead on the chessboard. Successful, tenured VCs will see even low-probability outcomes play out across their portfolios over time. In addition, pricing for private rounds involves small numbers of parties, so subjective factors and anchoring effects can have a 10x impact on final numbers.

Your best defense is to have an experienced party help protect your interests. When Mark Zuckerberg raised his initial outside capital from Peter Thiel, former founding CEO of PayPal, he had the benefit of Sean Parker's experience from founding Napster. As a result, they successfully negotiated for control for Zuckerberg, which he retains over Facebook to this day, and for pro-founder structures such as Series FF stock.

Overall, the most important factors to negotiate for in rank order include voting control, percentage ownership, price, board composition, capital raised, and liquidation preferences—assuming there are no exotic terms introduced by the buying or selling parties.[14]

Control matters even to innovators in large enterprises. The more control you have, the more likely you'll be able to bring your product vision to life.

From personal experience across two companies and other examples I've discussed with founders, I've seen each level of the triangles have as much as an order of magnitude impact. As a result, strategically managing the Innovation, Value, and Ownership Triangles can have a 1,000x impact on your final outcome.

The stakes are high, but these nested triangles will help you understand and order what is most important.

---

14   You can find definitions for many of these terms in the glossary.

CHAPTER 5:

LEARNING SLOW AND FAST

THE WORLD HAS finally met its first mad scientist: Elon Musk.

Elon Musk is a Dickensian figure. He's tall and imposing but with an oddly boyish face. His expressions bear faint traces of scars from his past, suffering he endured growing up in the chauvinistic, violent world of South Africa. He seems to balance that well, however, with Amber Heard or some other such actress on his arm.

Musk's ambition and reach know no bounds. He makes Google's famous moonshots look unambitious by *literally aiming for Mars.*

In addition to rockets (SpaceX), his current and prior companies produce electric cars (Tesla), solar tiles (SolarCity), and electronic payments (PayPal). He's now boring tunnels to battle traffic (the Boring Company) and investing in technology to turn us into cyborgs (Neuralink), all the while combating the specter of AI gone wild (OpenAI).

If there's anyone who embodies the spirit of "you can do anything if you put your mind to it," it's Elon Musk.

In a post on Reddit, Musk explains his approach to learning:

> It is important to view knowledge as sort of a semantic tree—make sure you understand the fundamental principles, i.e. the trunk and big branches, before you get into the leaves/details or there is nothing for them to hang onto.

I agree, although I describe it a little differently. I've often been asked the question: How does an English major end up founding multiple software companies? The answer is the Internet.

In 1999, when I founded Avamar, I learned primarily by searching the Internet with Yahoo. In 2008, when I founded Delphix, I used Google.

It sounds ridiculous, but it's true.

BUILDING FRAMEWORKS

The Internet has too much information. There are too many articles on too many subjects with varying degrees of expertise and correctness. Our brains can't index the information like the PageRank algorithm. What we can do, however, is critically interact with what we learn.

As I mentioned earlier, I started grappling with the information in the technology world by Thinking Big. I naturally gravitated toward the most critical factors in the data storage industry, focusing first on the economics and trade-offs of the different types of storage media, things even a neophyte could comprehend.

That knowledge helped me build a frame of reference. From there, I began reading white papers about how different storage technologies worked. Abstract, foreign concepts appeared everywhere, but I took the time to understand them, a process I call

Learning Slow. You might picture it as a slow-motion game of Whac-A-Mole.

As I filled in the frame of reference, I built a detailed framework that ultimately gave me the power of invention.

You'll know you've built a foundational framework for technical innovation when you can pass a series of self-administered tests. First, you can teach any of the core concepts to a reasonably intelligent person. Second, you can begin assembling the logical "Lego blocks" into new combinations. Third, you know the assembled Lego blocks will work without having to ask an "expert." Fourth, you can engage with experts in the field in a high-speed collaborative interchange as an equal.

Once you've built a foundational framework, streams of information that used to flow past you as too much unordered information will sort and fill in parts of the framework, building an ever-growing foundation that continues to accelerate your rate of learning.

The more you *really* learn, the more you will retain what you read, from meetings, and from conversations with other experts. This is the second phase of the process, which I call Learning Fast.

In addition, frameworks let you fill in the blanks from any direction. Any time I came across a potential competitor for Avamar or Delphix, I could take a glance at their technology or the functions of their product online and determine their competitive strengths and weaknesses. Or conversely, if they tried to hide their technology beneath layers of high-level product marketing, I could determine how their products worked by looking at their features and benefits.

A prerequisite for Learning Slow and Fast with frameworks is a certain caliber of intellect and a certain attitude.

I believe there is no field too complicated for me to master, and you should believe the same for yourself.

IN VINO VERITAS

The American wine industry is terrible, which makes for an incredible Value Seam.

The average American walks into a bar, pays $10 for the house wine, and gets a glass of something that makes her brace before she swallows. The average French or Italian walks into a bar, pays $3, and enjoys a well-balanced house wine.

Buying wines in restaurants, wine shops, or grocery stores is like spinning the Wheel of Misfortune. You don't always know if the $30 you pay will taste like $30 or $5. But you know for certain it will not taste like $50.

With a little technology, you could replace the fog of value with transparency and upend the industry, easily doubling the dollar value for wine for the average American. That's a window into Thinking Big about wine.

Wine is perfect for illustrating the power of learning frameworks. With all the different winemakers in all the different regions and all the different varietals, drinking wine can feel like a river of information flowing by you with little appreciable increase in knowledge or understanding no matter how much you drink or read.

Unless you have a framework.

To build a framework, there are five elements to taste in wine:

1. Fruit (tastes like … different fruits)
2. Alcohol (tastes like … vodka or other alcohol)
3. Acid (makes your mouth water and tastes like lemon juice)

4. Tannin (makes your teeth feel dry and tastes like bitterness from tea)
5. Terroir (tastes like minerals, rocks, or different types of earth)

There are also three phases to judging a wine:

1. The nose (smelling it in the glass)
2. On the palate (what it tastes like in your mouth)
3. The finish (the lingering taste in your mouth after the wine is gone)

Rating

ELEMENTS		
Fruit		86%
Alcohol		55%
Acid		85%
Tannin		70%
Terroir		32%

PHASES		
Nose		97%
Palate		48%
Finish		70%

That's enough to provide a basic framework for judging wines. Now, the next time you taste a good wine, you can judge it by these factors and remember the winemaker and varietal. If you happen to taste a great wine, place it, like a skyscraper, at a certain height in your mental framework.

A little hint: If the finish is long, balanced, and pleasant, it's a good wine. If the wine falls apart at the finish or if it tastes at all unpleasant in your mouth, then it's mediocre.

Always judge a wine by its ending.

Each wine you taste after your first great wine should be placed into a different sector (whites, reds, cabernet, merlot, French, American, etc.) and at a different mental height relative to your first great wine. Instead of each glass of wine disappearing after you drink it, each glass, each article, and each review will now be accretive, quickly building out your knowledge of wine.

Finally, there are eight factors you need to get right to maximize the quality of the wine you drink:

1. Right winemaker
2. In the right region
3. In the right vintage (year)
4. Stored for the right amount of time (years)
5. In the right conditions (dark, cold, not too dry, no vibration)
6. Served at the right temperature (depends on type of wine)
7. In the right glass (RIEDEL)
8. Paired with the right food

Quality

Factor	Quality
Winemaker	95%
Region	65%
Vintage	80%
Duration Stored	98%
Condition Stored	52%
Temperature Served	90%
Glass	68%
Food Pairing	78%

Each individual factor can have a significant (10%–100%) impact on the quality of wine you enjoy. Aligning these eight planets is a rare event for the average wine drinker (and even for the advanced).

As you build a framework, you actively grapple with concepts and trends, ordering them and layering frame upon frame until you have an elegant latticework that can easily sort details and facts. As you test and strengthen your frameworks, they will get tighter and more concise, and they should begin to snap into place. In wine, for instance, you just need to remember to align the eight planets to maximize quality and that there are five factors to taste in wine, across three major phases.

There is no deep learning without active struggle. Passive learning results in encyclopedic information, which is lacking in knowledge and wisdom and easily lost over time.

With a large Value Seam, the right framework, and the right technology, the wine industry is ready to be digitally harvested. So, that's enough about wine.

Once you build a framework in technology and software, you have an incredible advantage in *any* industry. Every field today is being refactored by the digital era. Here's the basic equation:

LEGACY INDUSTRY + DIGITAL ERA = DIGITALLY REFACTORED INDUSTRY

Companies operating across legacy industries are waking up, realizing often too late they need to become software companies—that they actually work in *my* industry.

Marc Andreessen wrongly asserted that every company is a software company. Every company is about to be *eaten* by a software company—even the software companies.

Time to get a drink.

CHAPTER 6:
DISCONFIRMATION BIAS

A T THE GALLERIA dell'Accademia in Florence, Italy, a series of rough-hewn stones line a long, elegant corridor. Looking closer, figures begin to emerge from the stone. Muscular forms struggle to break free from layers of marble, the turgescence of veins faintly visible.

These partially completed pieces, called *I Prigioni*, or *The Prisoners*, capture Michelangelo's evolving process of creation.

Great sculptors have the power of the artist's vision, an ability to see the masterpiece trapped inside a block of freshly quarried marble.

At the end of the corridor, we see the finished result. *David* stands nearly 17 feet tall above a marble plinth, his sling over his shoulder, his enlarged right hand casually at his thigh.

According to John Shearman, my professor at Harvard and one of the world-renowned experts on Michelangelo, the artist captures David just before he slays Goliath, a hint of anxiety on his chiseled face.

Today, we watch David and his digital sling slay legacy Goliaths with increasing regularity. *The Prisoners* and *David* capture the innovator's journey in sculpted marble.

The successful process of creation, of invention and execution, requires the active destruction of all that you do not know, all the rough marble that lies between the innovator and the masterpiece.

Entrepreneurs pitch me their ideas all the time. Most of them are ill equipped for the critical feedback they need to hear. They want happy talk. They want the supportive affirmation, validation, and confirmation they get from their friends, families, and colleagues.

Happy talk is for future failures.

I grew up with an antiauthority mindset, so I've been a skeptic all my life. That skepticism cuts both ways, for what I learn from others and from what I think I know.[15]

I have no pride in my own ideas. I care only about the *best* idea.

I have conviction in my beliefs, due to the strength of my informational frameworks. As a result, I act quickly and confidently, not hesitantly and timidly. Yet I will move instantly to a new position with new, contradictory information or a new, incisive point of view (POV).

I've been told that arguing with me can feel like a boxing match with the Blob. As soon as I hear a valuable, contrary point, it becomes part of my position.

I'm hardly alone in this.

Tim Cook, CEO of Apple, said of Steve Jobs, "He would flip on something so fast that you would forget that he was the one

---

15   The irony, of course, is that this book is filled with what I think I know. But we can dismiss that for now because you're still reading.

taking the 180-degree polar position the day before. I saw it daily. This is a gift, because things do change, and it takes courage to change. It takes courage to say, 'I was wrong.' I think he had that."

Jason Fried, the cofounder of Basecamp and coauthor of *Rework*, shared a similar observation from Jeff Bezos, when asked about his leadership principle that leaders "are right a lot." To be "right a lot," leaders can't be obsessed with only one POV. They have to be willing to revise their understanding and reconsider what they already know.

In his sometimes rambling, often insightful book, *The Black Swan*, Nassim Nicholas Taleb tells the tale of the turkey. Imagine a turkey waking up each morning, eagerly looking forward to breakfast from a kind, reliable human provider. For a thousand days, the turkey's conviction about the goodness of caretakers increases—until a third Thanksgiving season arrives. Gobble, gobble.

Even our greatest convictions can be wrong (all swans are white … until we find a black one). For the legacy chief and the innovator, it's imperative we see the farmer's POV if we want to survive.

FAULT FINDERS

I've raised more than $150 million from over 10 VCs. I personally know seven billionaires, worth more than $20 billion collectively, who have invested in my companies, as individuals or through their firms. That's what marketing looks like from the far side of a little success.

The reality looked quite a bit uglier for a twenty-something with an English degree trying to get his first software company funded in 1999 as the dot-com bubble burst around me.

In one of the great ironies of my career, 100 percent of the smaller, lesser-known "B tier" VC firms rejected me. It wasn't until I pitched five of the top ten VCs in Silicon Valley that I received term sheets from three.

Once you've developed a sufficient framework and you've reached the fast point in the technology learning curve, you'll have the credibility to begin building your network. I asked the smartest, most connected people I knew to connect me with the smartest, most connected people they knew. Within three degrees, I reached my first VC pitch.

VCs work hard for deal flow, to get access to a high volume of quality startups to fund. They also like to maintain optionality, so they will often tell you what more they'd like to see before they move forward—known as a "soft pass." Many will provide you with feedback, most of it encouraging. It's the rare bird that will tell you to your face what they say behind your back to their partners.

But that's the information you need the most. You need the flip side of the soft pass.

I like to read faces. It's partly why I had a second major in college: psychology. If you're observant and watch minute changes in facial expressions, you can actually see the cloud of critical thoughts forming on the faces of your audience.

Ask for the bald-faced, candid, hard feedback, and thank them for it.

Willingness to change your mind on new evidence, however, is only a half step. Take it the full step.

Charlie Munger, Berkshire Hathaway's vice-chairman and Warren Buffett's partner in crime (they make money from investing so easily it should be considered a crime), once explained Charles Darwin's philosophy:

One of the great things to learn from Darwin is the value of extreme objectivity. He tried to disconfirm his ideas as soon as he got 'em. He quickly put down in his notebook anything that disconfirmed a much-loved idea. He especially sought out such things. Well, if you keep doing that over time, you get to be a perfectly marvelous thinker instead of one more klutz repeatedly demonstrating first-conclusion bias.

When I first started pitching to VCs, I lacked depth and refinement in my understanding of building a business. Even though I could answer questions about the market and the technology that could exploit the Value Seam, I had lumps of unchiseled stone when it came to go-to-market strategy, managing teams, and hiring executives.

By attacking what I didn't know, by taking a hammer and chisel to what I thought I understood, I learned, quickly. By my third pitch, I had a reasonable command of the product and the business. By the seventh, I had a term sheet.

The standard VC pitch deck is an excellent framework for ensuring you know what you need to know at a high level, even if you're an innovator at a large company and don't need VC financing. Once you've assembled it, pitch it to the most evolved person you know in the technology industry and ask for the hard feedback.

Here are slides to include:

1. Company Vision and Mission (no more than a title and subtitle)
2. Problem and Pain in the Market (Value Seam)
3. Solution (Product Vision) and Use Cases
4. Market Trends that give rise to your opportunity

5. Market Size (TAM, SAM, SOM)
6. Competition (Differential Value)
7. Product Features and Development Roadmap
8. Business Model and GTM Strategy
9. Team
10. Financials (P&L, balance sheet, cash flow, cap table, deal summary)[16]

Don't wait passively for contrarian information to float into your field of view. The key is to find fault like a self-directed, heat-seeking missile.

The best Fault Finders are founders and CEOs who have successfully built a rocket ship in your space.

Operate confidently on what you currently think. But *always* sit on the same side of the table as the best idea.

LEAN IS DEAD

You can and should learn everywhere. But time is the enemy. And the enemy is getting shorter tempered as the Innovation Cycle continues to accelerate.

The Lean Startup Method and Customer Development didn't apply to me. And they continue to fail for thousands of startups and enterprise innovation programs when you look at sustained, high failure rates.

Lean suffers from two fatal flaws. First, it suffers from survivorship bias. Of the thousands of entrepreneurs that launch startups, some small percentage will succeed. Of the ones that succeed, some percentage will have to iterate or pivot their way to success. If you

---

16   You can find definitions for some of these terms in the glossary.

ask the survivors who iterated with customer feedback, they can look back at their experience and say it worked.

But what about the large percent that failed, even while iterating? And what about the other group that didn't need to iterate?

Lean is a siren song, encouraging entrepreneurs and enterprise innovators to dash their heads on the rocky shores of reality. Backtracing the success of a few survivors confuses cause and effect. And it doesn't help you predict or invent the future.

I'm not saying don't talk to customers. I talk to customers and learn from customers all the time. I've been talking to customers in a selling capacity for two decades.

The problem is that it's a struggle to get access to customers, especially if you're starting out and have nothing to sell but a concept. It takes time and effort to book a series of customer meetings. Even if you're an innovator in a large company, customer interactions are often heavily guarded to protect short-term revenue opportunities. As a result, you run into the second fatal flaw: small sample bias.

Whatever limited number of customer responses you gather, it's unlikely to be a statistically significant representation of the market. The data and your impressions will be dominated by the few most vocal and clearest customer voices, who only represent their large or small segment of the market.

Even worse, the questions you ask and the process you use are highly subject to confirmation bias—looking for data that confirms what you already think or asking questions that lead customers to provide data that confirms what you already think.

The key is to develop the mental frameworks and discipline that enable you to see clearly. Once you have that discipline, customer reviews can trigger insights that add incredible value.

With time as the enemy, the first order is to quickly find concentrated criticism to compress the learning cycle.

And as I've mentioned before, there is no greater concentration of learning than successful founders and CEOs who have built and launched a rocket ship.

They not only compress all the hundreds or thousands of meetings they have had with customers but also provide the two most precious commodities in driving innovation: insight and judgment.

CHAPTER 7:

THE TREE OF INNOVATION

D URING THE CAMBRIAN Period of evolutionary history, necessary conditions were met for oxygenation, seawater composition, and nutrient availability, resulting in an incredible diversification of new animals emerging on planet earth over a brief period. Speciation increased by more than an order of magnitude compared to the prior period.

Evolutionary biology occurs in fits and spurts.

Over the last decade, the necessary preconditions have been met to support a diversity of fast-growing and far-reaching apps. These preconditions include the rise of mobile and cloud comput-ing, and the series of platforms that have reached a supercritical mass of users. iOS, Android, Facebook, and Chrome all reach over a billion users and provide open application programming interfaces (APIs) for developers.

In biology, Charles Darwin traced the radiation of species in a map called the Tree of Life. In technology, there's a digital equivalent I call the Tree of Innovation.

While nonpractitioners of innovation, such as Nassim Nicholas Taleb, call the rise of disruptive technologies unpredictable black swans, the reality is quite a bit less mysterious.

Innovation can be highly and repeatedly predictable.

BOTTOM-UP DISRUPTION

Clayton Christensen's *The Innovator's Dilemma* describes how industry leaders repeatedly lose to new entrants who build simpler solutions, targeting a small, neglected segment of the market, and then add features and move upmarket over time.

In the end, the new entrant overthrows the complacent king, who has spent too much time delivering incremental features at the behest of a few large customers. Overly complex products enable the incremental monetization of large accounts. But they also create a formidable hurdle to adoption for novice users in new, underserved markets.

Try using a mature software product, such as Adobe Photoshop, for the first time. The rich feature set accosts you at the outset, and you feel instantly lost, unsure how to proceed and in which direction. That's what a user experience hurdle feels like—the opposite of the Google search experience.

The first users of Adobe Photoshop, however, enjoyed a different experience. With only the core features available, they situated themselves more quickly and efficiently.

Saleforce.com is a great example of Christensen's disruption. Benioff initially targeted startups and small businesses with a far simpler solution, a freemium trial, and a subscription pricing model. Over time, Benioff added features and moved up market, overthrowing Siebel as the market king.

As illustrated earlier, Salesforce.com is an example of business model and go-to-market innovation, more so than technical innovation. But there are many companies that are built on true, technical innovation, as we will soon see.

Companies around the world refer to Christensen's *The Innovator's Dilemma* when they talk about digital disruption. In reality, he covers only a single branch of the Tree of Innovation.

We'll cover a far wider series of branches in this chapter.

Easier to Use, 80/20 Features

RAIDERS OF XEROX PARC

You don't have to invent the future if someone has already invented it for you.

Andreas Bechtolsheim recounted how he started his career. As a PhD student in electrical engineering at Stanford in the late 1970s, he provided unpaid consulting at Xerox's Palo Alto Research Center (PARC), just a short drive from the university campus. According to Andy, walking into the innovation lab felt like "walking into the future."

In the '70s, IBM dominated computing with their massive, centralized mainframe computers. Xerox PARC, however, had invented desktop computers with graphical user interfaces. They also had keyboards, mice, and network-attached printers.

Andy's life changed forever when he was introduced to a winding cable with two plastic connectors at each end that serviced a network protocol called Ethernet.

At Stanford, he designed a workstation with built-in networking, which eventually grew into a company called Sun (Stanford University Network) Microsystems.

Bill Gates and Steve Jobs also raided Xerox PARC, long before they launched their famous companies.

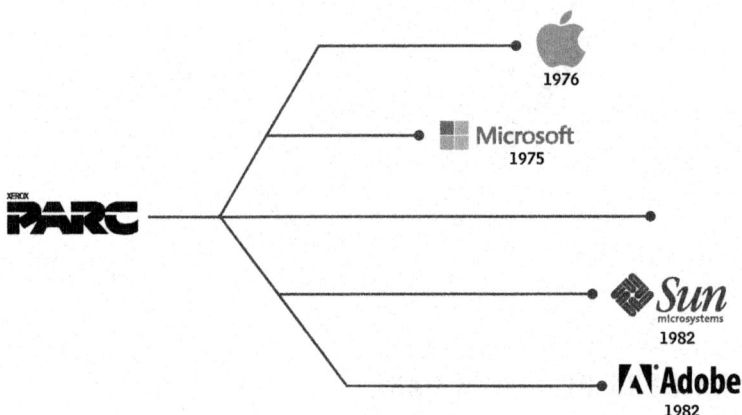

In a legendary interchange that has become part of Silicon Valley lore, Jobs once shouted at Gates about Windows: "You're ripping us off! I trusted you, and now you're stealing from us!"

Gates parried, "Well, Steve, I think there's more than one way of looking at it. I think it's more like we both had this rich neighbor named Xerox and I broke into his house to steal the TV set and found out that you had already stolen it."[17]

---

17   Apple actually licensed technology from Xerox PARC.

Xerox PARC gave rise to many of technology's biggest companies, including Apple, Microsoft, Sun, and Adobe.[18] These companies monetized *trillions* of dollars from the inventions they discovered there and form the Branch of Imitation.

As Pablo Picasso once said, "Good artists copy. Great artists steal." Jobs and Gates were great digital artists.

PLATFORM CONVERGENCE

After Benioff established the power of converting data center applications into software-as-a-service (SaaS) businesses, it still took years for the broader industry to repeat the innovation:

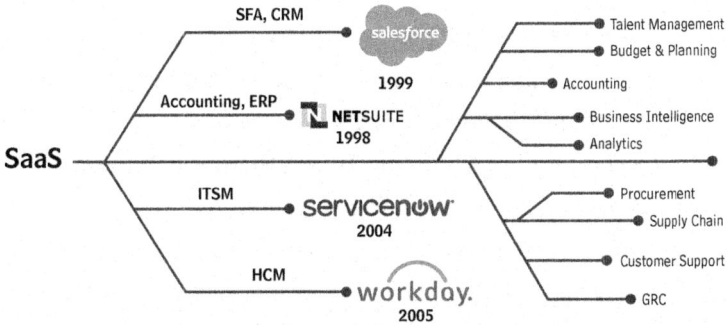

The real technology innovation came from the maturity of networks and the Internet, enabling SaaS companies to cost-effectively and reliably reach a large-enough and growing market of customers—the SaaS Value Seam.

As major technology trends mature, they open new avenues to new markets *over time*.

In daily life, we look forward or downward most of the time.

---

18   Xerox did monetize a few hundred million dollars from selling the printer technology developed at PARC, a relative pauper's share of the trillions in value they created for the technology industry at large.

Surfers, however, look up at the horizon of oncoming swells (which explains novice neck strain after initial attempts). When it comes to technology markets, it's imperative to look up and to know when to paddle hard.

Too early and companies tire and miss the wave. Too late and the companies that catch the wave come crashing down on you.

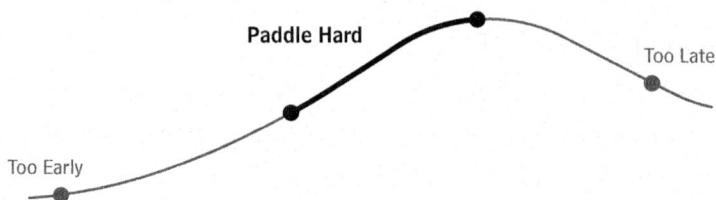

Benioff timed the development of the Internet-enabled market of customers just right, but it took *several years* for others to follow with the rest of the major enterprise apps.

In the end, this branch on the Tree of Innovation is best classified as an example of Platform Convergence.

In biology, convergent evolution occurs when similar types of species evolve due to similar environmental or selection pressures. For instance, dingoes and wild dogs, which have very similar features, emerged to fill the same beta predator position in Australia and Africa, two different biosystems.

When a new technology platform, like cloud computing, reaches maturity, the same types of applications that existed in the prior data center ecosystem have an opportunity to emerge in the next ecosystem.

New platforms emerge quickly, so Platform Convergence is a powerful concept for innovators to master. When a new platform emerges, look at successful products in past ecosystems and rebuild them on the new platform.

REGIONAL CONVERGENCE

Dingoes and dogs have an even closer parallel when we look at another branch of the Tree of Innovation: Regional Convergence. In the digital era, China has erected the Great Firewall, a government-enforced separation of their Internet from the rest of the world.

As a result, China has a regionally segregated digital biosystem. In their brave, isolationist world, we see an incredible convergence of Chinese apps that imitate American counterparts:

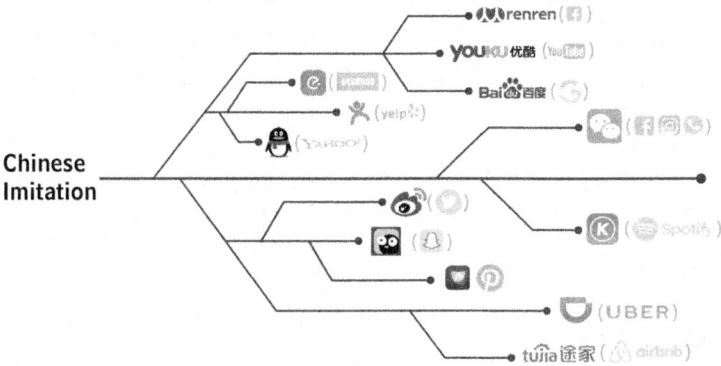

With different, isolated competitive dynamics, China has seen the rise of mega-Appzillas such as WeChat. Instead of having the key strategic technology world divided among the Apples, Alphabets, Amazons, and Facebooks, China has given rise to apex mega-predators.

WeChat initially imitated instant messaging companies in the United States but quickly integrated local commerce and payments, donations, gaming, stickers, transportation, and social media. Today, companies like Facebook race to consume the markets that WeChat has aggregated in an example of cross-regional convergence.

Innovators can study successes in other regions and then implement them in their own region.

TECHNOLOGY TRANSFER

At the very beginning of Avamar, after we invented how to eliminate duplicate blocks of data on disk by using a system of software pointers, I went back to Thinking Big. On a whiteboard, I mapped out all the areas where the technology could be applied. It could be applied to backup and recovery software, backup storage hardware, networking, and general data storage.

In the end, we picked one and developed new backup software. Over time, other companies entered the market and filled the other potential niches:

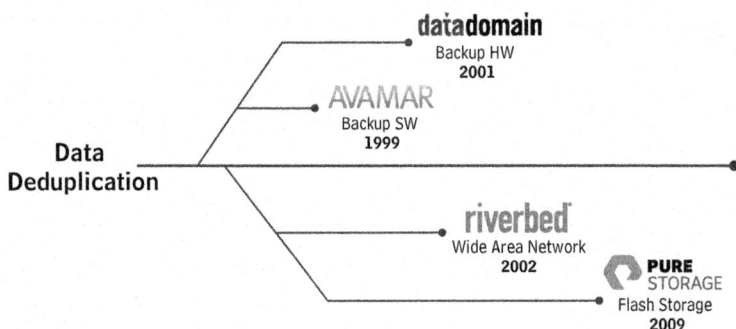

The technology world is filled with examples of Technology Transfer. In the early 1960s, IBM invented virtualization. Instead of providing each mainframe OS its own set of hardware, they used software to "trick" each OS into thinking it ran in its own hardware, while actually sharing one set of hardware underneath.

VMware later transferred this technology to the next-era platforms of PCs and distributed servers, in an example of Technology Transfer *and* Platform Convergence.

After VMware, a series of virtualization companies transferred the concepts to new markets:

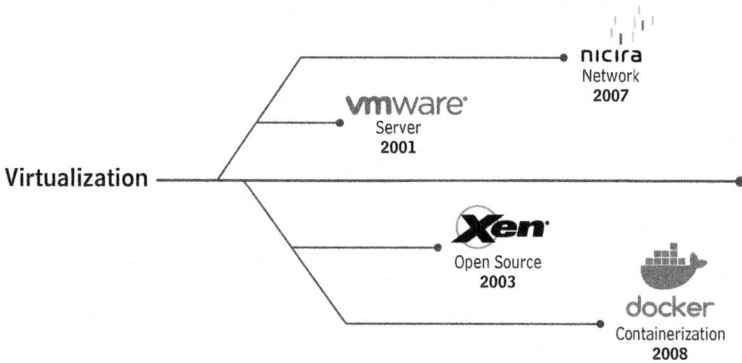

The financial services empire has been built on a moat of trust and relationships.

One of the most hyped technologies today is blockchain, a distributed, public, and digital ledger. With a digital public ledger, consumers no longer need to trust the long-established brands and reputations of old mainstays such as Bank of America, JPMorgan, or Wells Fargo. Due to its distributed nature, blockchain can ensure no single entity has the ability to control or destroy a public or shared transaction record.

As a result, blockchain has incited a swarm of FinTech startups to attack this venerable legacy industry:

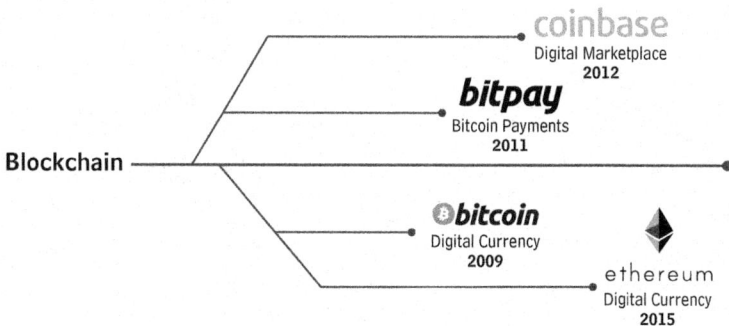

Here are other famous Branches of Technology Transfer:

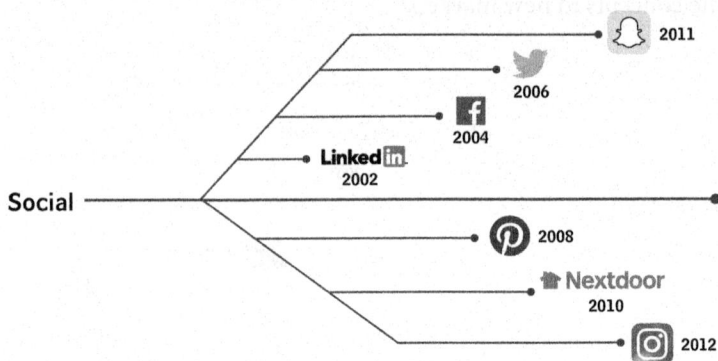

The next two are examples of both Business Model and Technology Transfer:

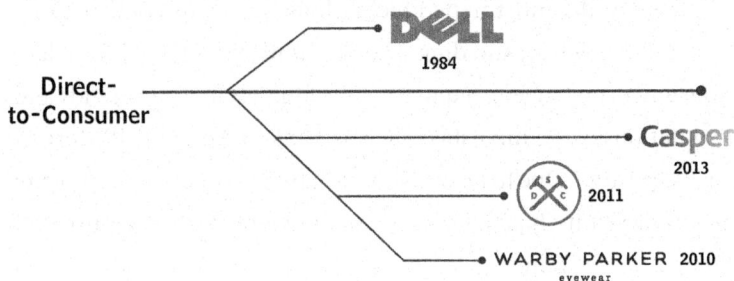

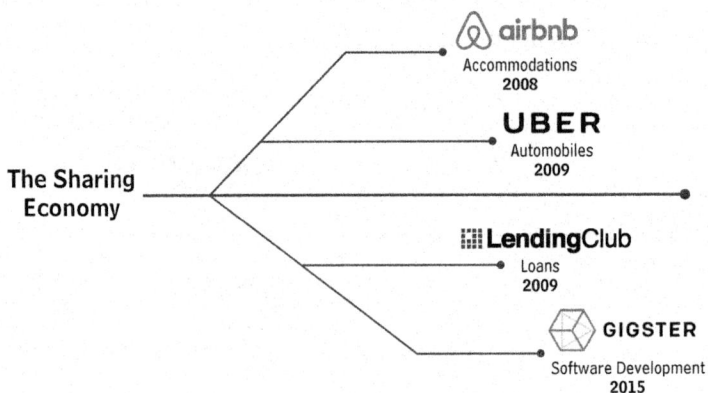

When major technologies emerge in one market, savvy innovators exploit them to win in new markets.

THE TALENT TRUNK

Joe Lonsdale is a Silicon Valley intellectual who throws a mean football, a transfer effect from playing pitcher in baseball and attending Stanford. I learned that when I played flag football at Levi's Stadium with Joe and a few of his buddies, including NFL Hall of Famers such as Ronnie Lott.

Joe recently founded 8VC, a firm that manages more than $2 billion in VC investments. He also cofounded Palantir, Addepar, and OpenGov. Palantir is the secretive analytics giant that reportedly helped find Osama bin Laden and was valued at $20 billion in a private financing round. Addepar has built a new data platform to transform wealth management, and OpenGov is digitally transforming government spending by providing a transparent financial app as a service.

Joe's accomplishments read like a long, fulfilling career in Silicon Valley. But he accomplished all of it by age thirty-five. How did someone so young achieve such a range of success in so little time?[19]

Joe started his career at the dead center of the Talent Trunk (see cross section on the right), the foundation for the Tree of Innovation. Talent supports, gives rise to, and weaves through the other branches we've covered.

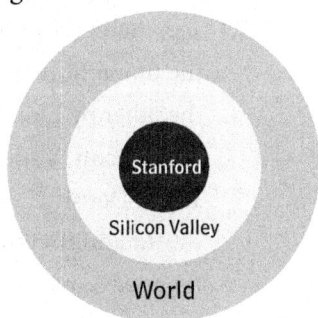

Stanford

Silicon Valley

World

---

19 Silicon Valley is littered with young entrepreneurs who have achieved one staggering success (e.g., Mark Zuckerberg), but multiple serial and concurrent successes at a young age are a rarity.

Silicon Valley is renowned as the epicenter of technology and digital transformation. Inside Silicon Valley, Stanford has the biggest and longest lineage of technology descendants:

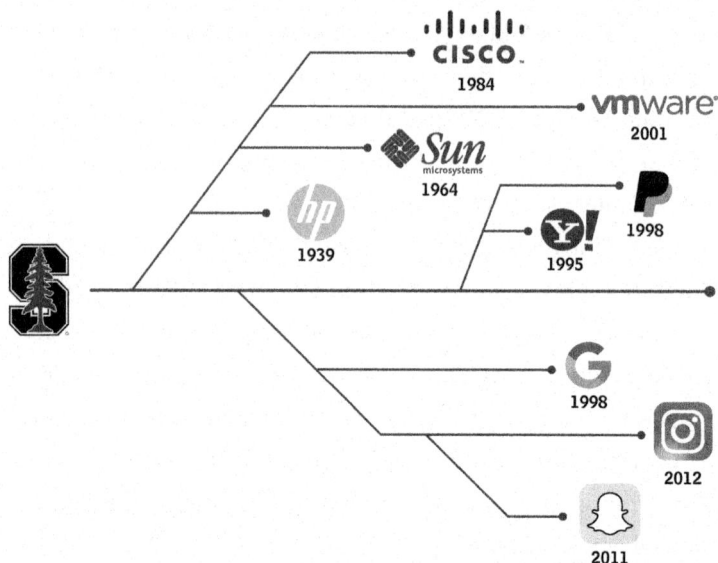

One of those descendants produced its own impressive lineage, famously known as the PayPal Mafia. PayPal resulted from the union of two payments startups, one founded by Peter Thiel, the other by Elon Musk.

Silicon Valley, Stanford, and PayPal tell a story about Talent Density.

In addition to Musk and Thiel, early PayPal employees later founded a string of technology successes. Reid Hoffman founded LinkedIn. Jeremy Stoppelman and Russel Simmons cofounded Yelp. Jawed Karim, Chad Hurley, and Steve Chen cofounded YouTube. David Sacks founded Yammer (acquired by Microsoft for $1.2 billion).

That list doesn't even include the PayPal employees who later founded *multiple* companies.[20]

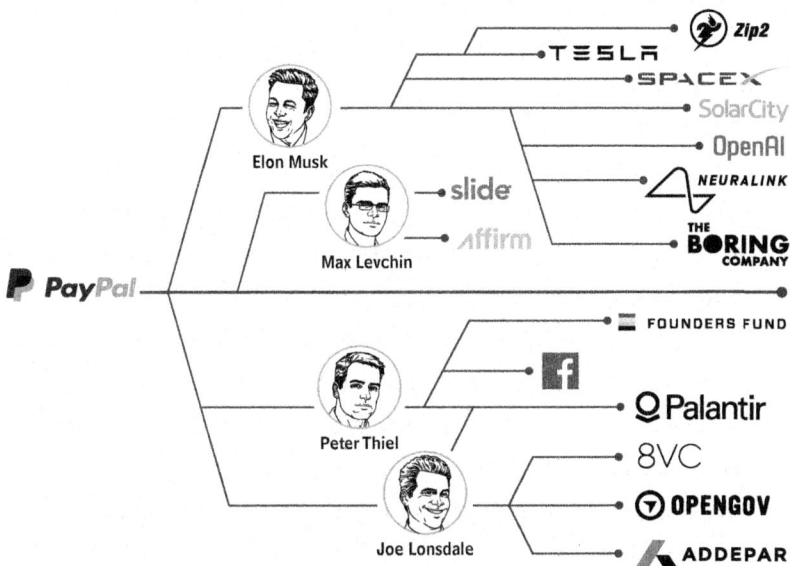

Those who think great technology companies are just the lucky animals (e.g., Nassim Nicholas Taleb) don't understand the incredible amount of repeatability the best entrepreneurs have in building companies.

If luck was the arbiter of success, the PayPal Mafia would be the meteorological equivalent of lightning striking the same location more than ten times in succession.

And PayPal hardly has the market cornered for success factories. The founding CEOs of Siebel, Salesforce.com, and Riverbed all worked for Larry Ellison at Oracle. The founders of Twitter

---

20   Facebook is depicted in Peter Thiel's branch, but he was the first outside investor, not technically a founder. A founding CEO's contribution as an investor and board member, however, can be very significant.

went on to found Square and Medium. And Steve Jobs famously founded NeXT, then acquired Pixar, and finally returned home to remake Apple.

Even at Delphix, early employees who worked closely with me have gone on to become founders of five new technology companies.

We can learn a lesson here by looking again at the history of biological evolution. Three million years ago, long after the breakup of Pangaea, the Isthmus of Panama connected North and South America.

For the first time, animals that evolved separately on two continents collided in the great American biotic interchange.

The result: Animals from the more competitive ecosystem dominated animals from the less competitive ecosystem. Deer, cougars, and their ilk drove the mass extinction of glyptodonts and terror birds.

The larger and more competitive arena bred stronger and more adaptable animals.

This is one of the subtle, lesser-known advantages of Silicon Valley. It is the largest, most competitive arena for technical innovation. And it has the highest density of talented technologists.

Joe was "just a kid" at PayPal and "doesn't get any credit" for the success there. But he watched a talented cast of innovators at work, built a series of frameworks for solving the challenges that meet startups at every turn of scale, and worked on a critical problem for the company that led to the cofounding of Palantir.

One of my great mistakes at Avamar was founding it in Southern California. Two years later, a competitor followed us into the market in Silicon Valley. In the end, we were acquired for $165 million and they were acquired for $2.4 billion—by the same company.

That 15x differential in exit is largely the result of the differential in Talent Density and why I later moved up to Silicon Valley for Delphix.

If you can't get the talent to move to you, move to the talent.[21]

Great innovators take advantage of Talent Density to magnify their opportunity and increase their chances of success.

---

21   Or open an office where you can find the talent you need.

SUMMARY OF PART ONE: THE IDEA

As high technology continues to commoditize itself, innovation has become increasingly accessible, turning mundane ideas into Appzillas and shattering the false belief that innovation is limited to the tech elite—the Innovation Glass Ceiling. Innovation is the birthright of every woman and man.

As Silicon Valley's Inhibitor Feeders consume friction points for startups, the Innovation Cycle continues to accelerate. Legacy companies, or the unknowing walking dead, do not properly gauge the speed of the threat, especially when it comes to second-, fifth-, and nth-order effects.

Innovation is the product of Thinking Big (finding Value Seams) and Thinking Small (inventing products). The Innovation Triangle has three sides: product, business model, and go-to-market strategy. The Value Triangle judges the worthiness of innovation on three factors: market size, time to value, and value differential. Innovation should target markets greater than $100 million, deliver value in well under 1 year, and have at least a 1x value differential (if not 1,000x).

To ramp up quickly in any new sector, and EVERY sector is becoming a new sector, you need to Learn Slow and Fast, building frameworks that quickly become flexible foundations for creation.

Rather than surrounding yourself with happy talk, embrace a Disconfirmation Bias to learn quickly from any source, accelerating your evolution and adaptability.

Finally, the Tree of Innovation holds the branches and leaves of greatness. Innovation is highly repeatable and predictable. It is not an abstract, amorphous concept limited to the geek gods on digital Mount Olympus.

PART TWO:
THE BUILD

CHAPTER 8:
VISION

VISION SETS THE stage. Together with product and road map, it largely predetermines the range of your outcomes.

In 1960, Theodore Levitt wrote an article titled "Marketing Myopia" for the *Harvard Business Review*. His article challenged CEOs with a question: What business are you in?

Levitt believed most business failures could be attributed to a nearsighted focus on selling products and services, instead of what the customers want from products or services. He illustrated his point with the railroad industry.

Railroad owners didn't fail because transportation went away. They failed because they didn't understand they were in the transportation business.

As I mentioned earlier, the world is filled with companies learning the following equation the hard way:

**LEGACY INDUSTRY + DIGITAL ERA =
DIGITALLY REFACTORED INDUSTRY**

Let's revisit Levitt's example. Cars, trucks, and planes quickly eclipsed the railroad industry. But here's what the car industry equation looks like today:

AUTOMOBILES + RIDE-SHARING APPS AND AUTOMATION = TRANSPORTATION AS A SERVICE

If you're not competing on Transportation as a Service, you're falling behind and in danger of obsolescence—one of the reasons Ford fired its CEO in 2017.

In the digital era, Levitt's message not only applies to large, established companies, but it applies even more to innovators.

THE DATA CAPITALIST

I've built my technology career on data. So, I've thought a great deal about a vision for data:

> In the agricultural era, the key factors to control were land and water. Wealth and power accreted to those who held the land and controlled access to water sources and waterways.

> In the industrial era the factors were steel, oil, and gas. When adjusted for inflation, the oil and steel magnates of the American Industrial Revolution were the wealthiest men in the history of humanity.

> In the digital era, the controlling factors are computer infrastructure and data. If your software controls the flow and delivery of data, you have a key control point for the future.

That's a *vision* that provides context for the men and women who make up Delphix. It also sets the context for a *mission*.

Vision paints a future state. Mission defines how you'll achieve that future state:

Our mission is to liberate data and help companies accelerate innovation.

Over the last two decades, data volumes and demands have exploded. Today, companies need data from their applications for ongoing software development, to respond to legal and regulatory requests, to train staff, to provide analytics and business intelligence, to leverage AI algorithms, and to move applications to and from clouds.

Unfortunately, data is trapped in silos and deeply entangled in systems and applications. There's tremendous friction moving data from place to place, which is why we feel trapped in our current versions of our phones, our laptops, and our PCs.

It's why we can't simply use any device we have in our hands. It has to be *your* data in the new device. And it has to be your *most recent* data.

For enterprises, data friction is even stronger. Companies employ hundreds to thousands of applications to run their businesses. The data in applications grows 30% a year on average. In addition, applications have tentacles pulling data to and from each other, creating an intricate web of dependencies. Data is a critical asset but also a risk, housing sensitive information like customer names, credit card numbers, and health information.

Companies that better manage the flow of data will vastly outperform their peers and maintain their positions in the face of digital disruptors.

At Delphix, we liberate data with our Dynamic Data Platform, a platform that makes data fast, nearly free, and secure.

As a result, our customers ship software faster. They employ AI algorithms more liberally. They migrate to and from clouds in half the time. And they do it all without risking publicly damaging data breaches.

That's an example of a vision, mission, and product brief for Delphix. After product, vision is the most important thing to get right for the innovator. Once you have the right vision, it will naturally beget the mission.

To capitalize on data or any opportunity, you need a compelling vision. Your vision must inspire passionate, energetic, capable individuals to your cause—especially if you're innovating within a large enterprise. And it must keep them with you through the inevitable trials and tribulations along the innovator's journey.

SIZE MATTERS

When it comes to vision, size matters. No one wields a bigger vision than Elon Musk.

We put a man on the moon in 1969, at the height of the Cold War. After the decline of the Soviet Union, NASA fell from the pinnacle of the world's stage into an archaic, darkened technology basement.

It took until Elon Musk's arrival for rocket science to reemerge on the world stage. Musk's vision at SpaceX is "to enable people to live on other planets," a plan B for planet earth. Instead of sending people to the moon, Musk wants to colonize Mars.

There are limits to vision. Myopia is a risk, but presbyopia (farsightedness) is an equal risk. If you can't execute on the vision, it's not vision. It's vain ambition.

In 2008, Elon Musk was a single failed rocket launch away from catastrophically imploding. Tesla missed its shipment date (again) and was quickly hemorrhaging its remaining cash. The first three rockets launched by SpaceX had failed, one literally exploding, and the company could afford only one more attempt.

Musk had invested all his returns from Zip2 and PayPal, had convinced his family and friends to invest their savings, and was on the brink of bankruptcy.

If that fourth rocket had failed to launch, Elon Musk may never have recovered.

But it succeeded, and after some serious financial maneuvering, Musk convinced Tesla's investors to extend another round of financing as well.

Elon Musk sets the watermark for the pinnacle of vision: We need a plan B for planet earth.

Shoot any higher, and you're climbing on thin air.

Big visions are the stuff religions are made of. Over the course of human history, more good and harm has been done in the name of religion than any other organizing human force. Religions breed zealots: men, women, and children who are literally willing to die for the vision they believe.

While Musk and technology companies fall a little short of religious zealotry with their employees, it isn't for want of trying.

Now contrast that with the zombies you find sitting in cubicles across the world's office buildings. Do you want zealots or zombies behind you?

The difference comes down to vision.

REALITY DISTORTION?

In 2012, I made several trips down to Facebook's new headquarters on 1 Hacker Way, Menlo Park, California. Facebook had successfully deployed Delphix to accelerate several corporate app programs.

You could already see, hear, and feel the belief and fervor employees had in their company's vision. This was before they went public, before they had a billion monthly active users, and well before their role in Trump's election to the White House.

After I got back from their office, I recounted the tale to a friend: "They really believe they are changing the world at Facebook."

She smirked and rolled her eyes. "What, by wasting everyone's time?"

I laughed. When I went to the Facebook app, I'd invariably spend my time scrolling through pictures from friends' vacations, skipping over videos of kittens and puppies, and ignoring requests to play *Mafia Wars*.

But with a market cap of $450 billion in 2017, ambitious programs to bring Internet connectivity to the world, and Mark Zuckerberg's massive donations to selected causes.... Who's laughing at their vision now?

PIED PIPERS

In the HBO series *Silicon Valley*, the protagonist names his company Pied Piper, after the German legend of a man who could lead children away from their families by playing his magic pipe. In real life, I've had the opportunity to meet a few digital Pied Pipers.

One of them is Bill Gates. In his seventies, Gates still exhibits an active, highly engaged mind. Gates shared a story about working with Steve Jobs on the Macintosh. Jobs wasn't CEO at the time and had limited resources at his disposal, but he could still get people to dance to his tune. It's a critical ability if you're an innovator in a large enterprise.

"I think I had more people working on the project than he did," Gates recalled. "But in the mornings, I would come in and check on what the engineers were working on, and they'd tell me, 'Steve said this' and 'Steve said that.' I wanted to shake them and say, 'Wake up, wake up!'"

Gates prided himself on being a bit of a Pied Piper, but in the face of Jobs and his legendary reality distortion field,[22] even his own employees found themselves at the mercy of a true pipe player.

In the end, a great vision is best embodied in a visionary storyteller, a modern Pied Piper.

The lesson? Invent your product, paint the biggest vision you can with it, and play your pipe to the best of your abilities.

---

22 At a teensy, weensy scale, I've had employees tell me I cast a reality distortion field, that everything looks great and optimistic when they speak with me, but all the work looks harder and more daunting the further away they get.

CHAPTER 9:
LEADERS AND ANTI-LEADERS

> Humpty Dumpty sat on a wall.
> Humpty Dumpty had a great fall.
> All the king's horses and all the king's men
> Couldn't put Humpty together again.
> —*English nursery rhyme*

WARREN BUFFETT HIRES for three traits: intelligence, energy, and integrity. He explains, if candidates "don't have the latter, the first two will kill you."

According to that rubric, Buffett would not have considered Mark Zuckerberg when he first started Facebook.

At the time, Zuckerberg surrounded himself with controversy. First, he launched a social ranking site resembling Tinder called Facemash. Within hours, Harvard revoked his network privileges and later brought him before the administrative board for potential expulsion.

Then he interviewed with the Winklevoss twins to help them develop their social networking site, only to sit on the project until he shipped his own.

After that, he executed a scheme to wrest sole control for himself by diluting his cofounder, Eduardo Saverin, who had personally bankrolled their initial expenses. Finally, he hired a president named Sean Parker, the infamous founder of Napster, a service shut down for illegally pirating music.

One of the great ironies of the technology world today is how such broken people can create such perfect products. And they're broken in myriad ways.

Steve Jobs famously rejected paternity for his daughter, even after a DNA test.

Despite his extraordinary wealth, he later refused to pay for her college tuition until neighbors decided to pay her way for him.

Exposé after exposé has revealed the inhumane treatment of employees at Amazon, where workers regularly cry at their desks, get stripped bare by stinging criticisms, and run scurrying for answers when they get Bezos's infamous support emails forwarded to them with a single addition: "?"

In addition to nearly ruining his own finances and those of his family and friends, Elon Musk demands tireless devotion to his causes. Employees regularly sacrifice their days and nights to make (and miss) his overly aggressive deadlines. And even his closest, most loyal lieutenants get callously tossed along the wayside if they get crosswise with the iron-fisted ruler.

They are all broken people. But they ship elegant, perfect products.

Travis Kalanick, Uber's former CEO, claims the Anti-Leader crown. His brash, aggressive leadership resulted in a series of bombshell revelations in 2017. Susan Fowler broke the first crack in the dam when she published a blog post revealing sexism and sexual harassment at Uber. Then came a viral video showing the billionaire Kalanick lashing out at a poorly paid Uber driver. Next was the Justice Department investigation of Greyball, an internal program designed to evade law enforcement.

Alphabet drove another crack into the dam when it sued Uber for trade theft for self-driving car technology. After that came the revelation of improper handling of information regarding the rape of a female Uber passenger. Finally, former US attorney general Eric Holder launched an internal investigation that resulted in more than twenty firings and ultimately Kalanick's resignation.

Anti-Leaders power the technology world. And the technology world rules the business world.

In *Good to Great,* Jim Collins explains that leaders need to build companies like "clock makers," with layered, enabling processes. He contrasts that with "time tellers," more limited leaders who direct execution rather than enable execution.

In addition, Collins outlines the "enlightened" narrative for today's leaders. A "Level 5 Leader" serves his company with humility and will.

But as the long list of Anti-Leaders proves, it's a false narrative for the digital era.

Anti-Leaders absolutely tell time. Anti-Leaders not only direct the action, but they often do detailed work themselves. Rather than lead with humility, Anti-Leaders such as Bezos publish leadership traits that openly say they want leaders that "are right a lot." Or like Musk, they are larger than life, overdemanding and overbearing.

Today's technology Anti-Leaders disprove the "enlightened" narrative and offer an important lesson to legacy chiefs.

ANTI-INNOVATOR BIAS

Boards and legacy chiefs need to wake up to today's reality.

Product visionaries come in all shapes and sizes, with varying degrees of integrity and maturity.

One of Collins's key points in *Good to Great* is "who before what." Great leaders get the "right people on the bus" before product development, strategy, or execution.

But Silicon Valley regularly ignores this "wisdom."

Young technology founders have such a negligible track record that there's no telling "who" they are. Venture capitalists regularly back founding CEOs in their twenties, who have little or no work history.

As a result, shrewd venture investors, such as Peter Thiel who funded Facebook, start with *what*. With its explosive virality already proven, Facebook made it easy to overlook any shortcomings of its CEO, including his early business cards:[23]

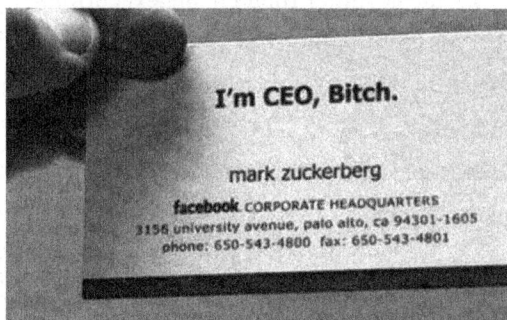

As legacy chiefs look for leaders to drive innovation, they need a pragmatic, patient, and prepared mindset. While you may not fully know or like the *who*, you must project who they

---

23   While the card and "title" existed, this may not be a picture of the actual version.

might become and try to positively influence the long road of personal growth.

Today, Mark Zuckerberg looks and sounds every inch the civic-minded leader we expect to head a top technology company.

What you want to avoid, however, is the call of the dark side for young Kalanicks in training.

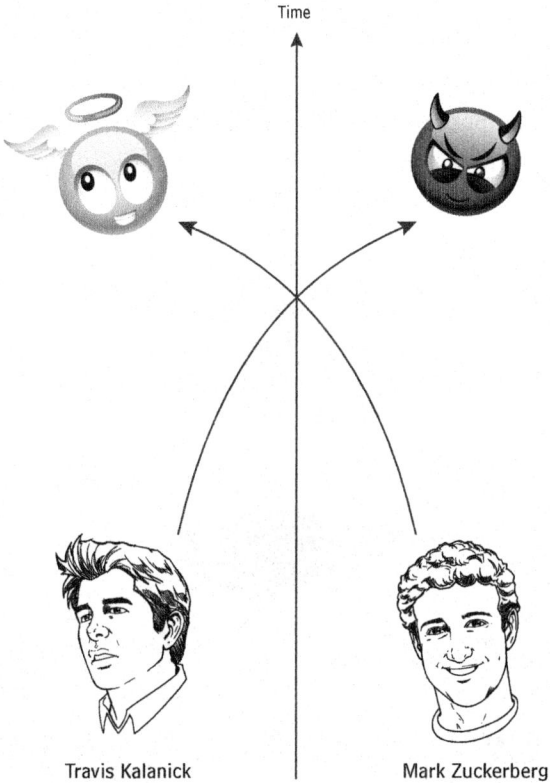

Travis Kalanick   Mark Zuckerberg

Innovation sometimes takes the form of an Anti-Leader. If you're a legacy chief and you miss a key opportunity presented by an Anti-Leader, you may have just sentenced your company to death in the market.

HOLY TRINITY

Robert Kraft is a considerate, caring, and perceptive human being. He's also the owner of the New England Patriots.

Robert gave me a ride on his private jet one day when we were both headed to Boston from New York. On the trip, I asked him about the secret of the Patriots' longevity at the top. Robert told me, "It helps to have the coach, quarterback, and owner in alignment."

In the salary cap era, the New England Patriots have been the most dominant team in the NFL, winning 14 division titles and 5 of the last 17 Super Bowls since Belichick became head coach in 2000.

Here's my diagram of the Football Trinity:

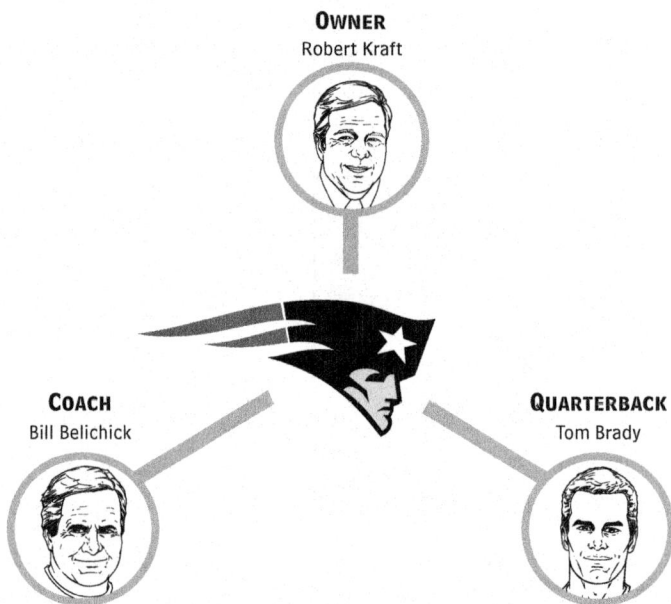

OWNER
Robert Kraft

COACH
Bill Belichick

QUARTERBACK
Tom Brady

Robert's insight instantly resonated with me. Having spent the last decade in the San Francisco Bay Area, I had recently watched the San Francisco 49ers take a dive into the NFL basement.

For a few years, the 49ers looked like they had the ingredients for a potential dynasty, with Jim Harbaugh as coach and Colin Kaepernick as quarterback.

Owners, however, set the tone and maintain the foundation.

When 49ers CEO Jed York decided to back his general manager over his coach, he cracked the foundation and effectively ran Harbaugh out of town. Kaepernick, who had emerged as a potential superstar under Harbaugh's tutelage, immediately went into a statistical nose dive, and the 49ers have been losing ever since.

Here's what it looked like, just before it all fell apart:

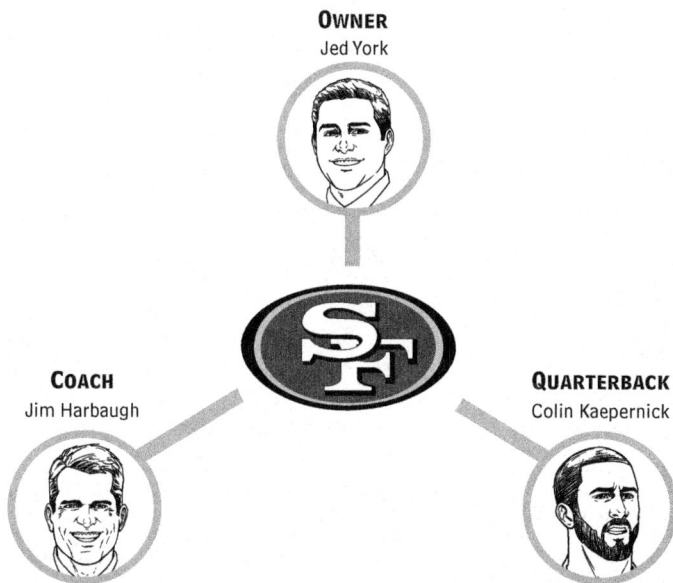

OWNER
Jed York

COACH
Jim Harbaugh

QUARTERBACK
Colin Kaepernick

Contrast that with the Patriots. Bill Belichick can probably melt asphalt with his trademark glare, but he has Robert's full, unwavering support. And while players might wilt a bit under Belichick, they pick themselves up and run the extra mile for the warmth and care of the Kraft family.

Robert's insight made me think about the digital equivalent, a digital union of the father, son, and holy spirit.

It's no accident that the world's greatest technology companies are led by CEOs that embody the Product Trinity—leaders that often play the role of de facto product manager, CTO, and head of user experience design.

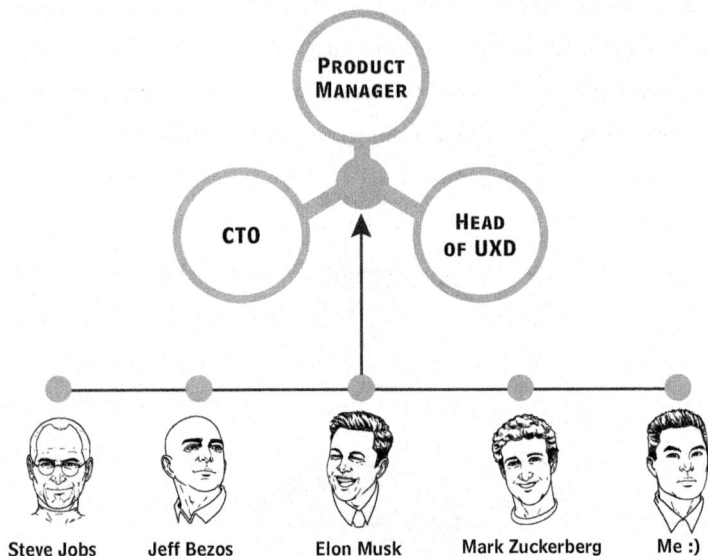

Steve Jobs   Jeff Bezos   Elon Musk   Mark Zuckerberg   Me :)

These leaders may have lieutenants reporting to them with those titles, but they actively do these jobs on a regular basis—determining actual, specific product requirements, making technology choices and setting technology direction, and designing details of the user experience.

WEEDS VERSUS SEEDS

I imagine legacy chiefs around the world muttering to themselves in disagreement, "I can't afford to be in the weeds. That's why I hire great leaders into the organization."

Jeff Bezos became the richest man in the world in 2017, running one of the top three companies in the world based on market capitalization. The other two companies are also technology companies.

In his 2017 letter to shareholders, Bezos shared his views on how to avoid the long, slow slide into obsolescence, what he calls "Day 2." One of his four key points includes this warning: "Resist Proxies."

Bezos writes, "Market research and customer surveys can become proxies for customers—something that's especially dangerous when you're inventing and designing products." He later explains, "A remarkable customer experience starts with heart, intuition, curiosity, play, guts, taste. You won't find any of it in a survey."

Bezos clearly has heart, intuition, curiosity, play, guts, and taste.

Steve Yegge, a former employee of Amazon, ranted on his blog:

Jeff Bezos is an infamous micro-manager. He micro-manages every single pixel of Amazon's retail site. He hired Larry Tesler, Apple's Chief Scientist and probably the very most famous and respected human-computer interaction expert in the entire world, and then ignored every goddamn thing Larry said for three years until Larry finally—wisely—left the company. Larry would do these big usability studies and demonstrate beyond any shred of doubt that nobody can understand that frigging website, but Bezos just couldn't let go of those pixels, all those millions of semantics-packed pixels on the landing page. They were like millions of his own precious children. So they're all still there, and Larry is not.

Of course, a series of movies and books have made famous Steve Jobs's obsession with the purity and simplicity of design, even demanding that the *inside* of his products look neat and elegant.

Jobs and Bezos weren't in the weeds. They understood that great design and great products are the *seeds* of the future.

When Microsoft's stock stagnated for a decade, the company replaced CEO Steve Ballmer with Satya Nadella. I met Nadella at a dinner event to discuss how Delphix accelerates the migration of enterprise apps to the cloud, including Microsoft's cloud, Azure.

Nadella has a very pronounced skull, not only because of his shaved hair but also because of the veins subtly protruding from his temples, actively feeding his highly analytical mind. A longtime employee of Microsoft, Nadella led the transformation of many of Microsoft's legacy technologies and services from on-premises to the cloud.

As CEO, he implemented a "cloud-first, mobile-first" strategy that overcame decades of internal political strife, resulting in all-time highs for Microsoft's stock price in 2017. He later updated the strategy to focus on AI, continuing to shadow the Alphabets and Amazons of the world.

He really became animated and passionate when the topic of augmented reality (AR) came up, describing his vision of what AR could do to improve knowledge-worker productivity, providing everyone with the magical, dynamic interfaces depicted in movies such as *Minority Report*.

If the CEOs of the world's biggest companies can afford to spend time on product requirements, technology decisions, and user experience, can the rest of the world's CEOs afford not to?

CHAPTER 10:
BUILT TO FAIL

TOM WEST STANDS calmly at the tiller, grinning in the dark, possessed by high spirits. All around him a terrible storm rages, while the seasoned crew huddles like refugees under the glow of running lights.

So opens *The Soul of a New Machine*, Tracy Kidder's Pulitzer Prize-winning book. The nonfiction account chronicles a skunk works project, headed by Tom West, that desperately tries to ship a next-generation computer before a competitor crushes them in the market.

When new executives joined my team, I often recounted this opening scene. Startups, by definition, are exercises in desperation. Ship product and prove Product-Market Fit before running out of cash. Raise another round and prove scalable unit economics before running out of cash. Even in the good times, even when you're winning, the storms of the market rage all around you.

I told our executives it's important to *enjoy* the storm. Do not get excited by the highs. Do not become distraught by the lows. Keep a calm hand on the tiller and eyes on the North Star—our vision and mission in the market.

Legacy chiefs, however, ride at the helm of a battleship.

They do not feel the forces of the market acutely. They do not act as if their small sailing vessel can be torn apart at any time.

But it's a false sense of security.

When Amazon first waded into the grocery business with delivery trucks and automated checkout in test stores, John Mackey, CEO of Whole Foods, called it Amazon's "Waterloo moment." Like the Webvans before them, Amazon would fail to digitize a market of national and local supply chains, where consumers like to touch and smell their produce.

That might have been true, until Amazon decided to eat Whole Foods for nearly $14 billion. Within hours of the news, the stock prices of the other major grocery chains tumbled downward beneath waves of market pessimism.

Amazon, of course, rode the market upward, its stock price rising by over $15 billion—*more than the cost of the acquisition.* The appreciation in Amazon stock arguably pays for the acquisition, making it essentially free for Bezos and company.[24]

As they grow, technology Appzillas will continue to expand their domains, toppling industry after industry after industry. Worse yet, their captains, like Dread Pirate Bezos, deeply embody the Product Trinity.

They make technology decisions fast. They understand the profound difference between weeds and seeds, and they're at a scale where they can eat legacy companies in their entirety, rather than disrupt them over time.

Now, let's look at how legacy companies compare.

---

24 They have plenty of cash, so they don't actually need to sell more stock or debt for the purchase.

ORGANIZED FAILURE

CEOs bear the power and responsibility for global resource allocation. As organizations scale, they learn how subtle cues can send ripples of consequences throughout their organizations. Those who are deft at organization and administration, hire and unify great teams, set focused strategies, and ensure disciplined execution often rise to the top of massive, established organizations. It's still not enough to survive the digital era.

In successful technology companies, the Product Trinity captains the ship or reports directly to the captain. In legacy companies, you need to excavate several layers of organizational structure before you find the first individuals who do the actual work of product managers (PMs), chief technology officers (CTOs), and heads of user experience design (UXD).

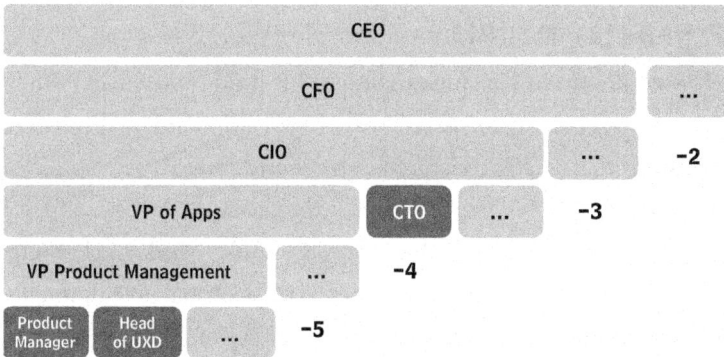

CEO				
CFO			...	
CIO		...	**−2**	
VP of Apps	CTO	...	**−3**	
VP Product Management	...	**−4**		
Product Manager	Head of UXD	...	**−5**	

There's an enormous divide between having the Product Trinity and a legacy chief at the top. Once a role such as PM falls more than three layers down into an organization (−3), it loses most of its visibility to a CEO.

As its importance and visibility falls, its power within the organizations weakens. At −3 or −4, a PM, CTO, or head of UXD falls victim to bureaucratic checks and balances. Key decisions now require peer reviews and departmental conflict checks.

Consensus rules. And consensus is the enemy of speed.

The weight of bureaucracy is the opposite of power at the top, where subtle emphasis often ripples down the chain. At −4 and below, it takes a herculean effort to impact an organization, or it's just impossible.

Yet the roles of the Product Trinity often report starting at −3 (CTO) and lower (−5 for head of UXD and PMs).

Compare that to Elon Musk, who personally spends 80 percent of his time on new product engineering and design.

If the digital era is refactoring every industry, you can't survive by suffocating the most critical roles under endless layers of bureaucracy.

FINANCIAL MYOPIA

How could Travis Kalanick maintain his hold on the CEO office for so long, enabling an incredible string of scandals and disastrous decisions that finally conspired to have him resign?

Control.

Like the Google founders and Facebook's Mark Zuckerberg, Kalanick and his cronies own a special class of shares with magnified voting rights, effectively cementing control of the company. The board at Uber, which includes many of Kalanick's largest shareholding investors, was relatively powerless, wielding only bare influence against his relentless will and aggression. It took a public unveiling and the accidental death of his mother to finally rein him in.

But boards and investors typically have far more power over legacy companies.

I had coffee with Sohaib Abbasi, former chairman and CEO of

Informatica, shortly after his public software company sold to a private equity firm for $5.3 billion. Sohaib is a technology statesman, well-dressed, grave in his demeanor, and reserved in his speech. He had a strong view of market trends, competitive threats, and what Informatica needed to do to continue growing in the market.

So why the sale?

When companies go public, institutional investors typically buy the lion's share of the float, the shares made available for sale to the public. By the time companies reach a scale large enough to go public, most of their highest annual rates of growth are behind them.

As a result, companies like Informatica build up a base of conservative institutional investors, including pension funds, endowment funds, mutual funds, insurance companies, commercial banks, and hedge funds.

These investors judge their investments on quarterly revenues, earnings, and operating expenses—a focus on short-term financials. If they don't like what they see, investors can become highly disruptive activists, agitating for mergers, acquisitions, divestitures, and sale to private equity or an acquirer. Chop, slop, or sale.

In a world where digital disruption is the only certainty, financial myopia ensures long-term obsolescence.

Contrast that with the big technology companies. In his first letter to shareholders, right after Amazon went public in 1997, Jeff Bezos gave clear notice to shareholders:

> We will make bold rather than timid investment decisions where we see a sufficient probability of gaining market leadership advantages. Some of these investments will pay off, others will not, and we will have learned another valuable lesson in either case.

Bezos has been true to his word ever since. The company has been run with a permanent long-term orientation, reinvesting cash flows back into growth at an unprecedented rate and scale for decades. With a constant focus on growth, Bezos has maintained an aggressive, future-minded investor base—tolerant of spending fortunes on trials in new markets, like the cloud.

Google later followed Amazon's lead, with a similar message to investors. They would not function like a "typical" company, and they would continue to invest in their business to maintain their competitive advantage as an Internet pioneer.

For companies to succeed over the long term, they not only need the Product Trinity at the helm, but they also need the right board and the right investors.

If you look at the board of a typical, venture-backed Silicon Valley startup, it consists of technology founders, venture capitalists who have built their careers around disruptive companies, and seasoned technology executives. In addition, the investors expect continued investment to drive growth.

Legacy companies need to evaluate their board and their investors if they want the support they need to survive.

Taken as a whole, the Product Trinity CEO, board composition, and investor support provide a clear report card for a company's prospects of surviving the digital era:

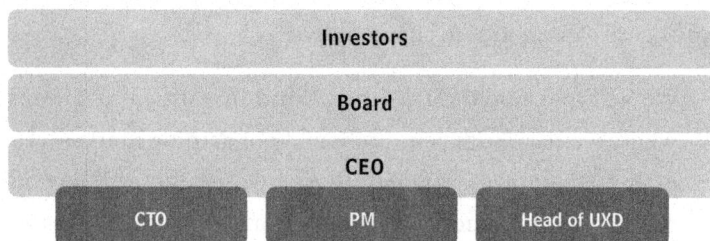

Investors
Board
CEO

CTO	PM	Head of UXD

Does your organization make the digital grade?

	GRADE
ORGANIZATION	**A**
A: CEO embodies the Product Trinity	
B: Trinity roles report directly to CEO	
C: Average of Trinity roles reports at -2	
D: Average of Trinity roles reports at -3	
F: Average of Trinity roles reports at -4 or more	
BOARD	**A**
A: All members have experience growing technology companies	
B: All but audit, compensation committee chairs	
C: Over half	
D: Under half	
F: One or fewer	
INVESTORS	**P**
Pass: Investor base supports a long-term digital strategy	
Fail: Investor base does not support a long-term digital strategy	

BEWARE YOUR STRENGTHS

GE is a cautionary tale.

Back in 2014, Jeff Immelt, former GE chairman and CEO, talked a great digital game: "If you went to bed last night as an industrial company, you're going to wake up this morning as a software and analytics company."

He clearly understood the digital imperative.

In addition, Immelt preached digital transformation internally and marketed it externally—conditioning employees, customers, suppliers, and investors in the strategy. GE's relentless commercials rebranded the company as the leader of the Digital Industrial Age, and Immelt set a public goal to become a "top ten" software company by 2020.

GE had a CEO committed to change.

In stark contrast, many of today's legacy companies have digital transformation being driven by their IT organizations, reporting up through a CFO or COO—far too low in the organization.

But with public support from the very top, how did GE's digital strategy go wrong?

After seeing the dazzling light shows and commercials, I peeled back the curtain and talked to GE's technology leadership. They took ownership for the $15 billion goal in annual software sales by 2020. But they decided they would first focus on the "low hanging fruit," reducing billions in operational spending by focusing on procurement and then proactive maintenance for their industrial machinery.

In other words, they were playing defense. But to win in the digital world, you need to play *offense*.

If Immelt had taken a dispassionate Disconfirmation Bias to his digital transformation program, he would have seen that GE's key programs were about cutting costs, rather than truly driving market innovation. He thought big and marketed big—playing to his strengths—but he lacked product vision.

He needed technology programs that would make a difference to an organization at the scale of GE. He needed great products in emerging Value Seams. And he could not afford to delegate the details of innovation to lower-level leadership that would think and act tactically.

In 2017, Immelt stepped down from his role due to tremendous shareholder and board pressure. The company had shed more than

$150 billion in market capitalization since he took office sixteen years prior.

He had reached the end of his digital runway.

FIRE YOURSELF

Intel initially built its empire manufacturing memory chips under founding CEO Gordon Moore. Moore observed that the number of transistors on a chip doubled every eighteen months or so, which became well known as Moore's Law. In the 1980s, however, Japanese firms mastered Moore's Law, destroying the margins and profits in the industry.

Moore had a pivotal conversation with Andy Grove, Intel president at the time. Grove tells the story in *Only the Paranoid Survive*:

> I looked out the window at the Ferris wheel of the Great America amusement park revolving in the distance, then I turned back to Gordon and I asked, "If we got kicked out and the board brought in a new CEO, what do you think he would do?" Gordon answered without hesitation, "He would get us out of memories." I stared at him, numb, then said, "Why shouldn't you and I walk out the door, come back and do it ourselves?"

Moore and Grove decided to fire themselves and walk back into Intel as the "new" CEO and "new" president.

They sacrificed their enormous advantages in memory and bet the entire company on a relatively insignificant new product: the microprocessor.

When IBM decided to use Intel's microprocessors in its PCs, Intel, as we know it today, was reborn.

Silicon Valley has a long history of CEOs brave enough to abandon positions of primacy. After destroying Blockbuster's tape and DVD rental business, Netflix's Reed Hastings saw that streaming video would obviate the movies-by-mail business that made Netflix a household name. So he fired the CEO of that business and walked in as the CEO of a digital streaming business. And he did it again when Netflix became a content creator.

With innovation cycles accelerating, CEOs need to move fast and with great certainty. They cannot rely on process and leadership teams to outexecute and outflank competitors in the market.

You cannot market your way to survival. You cannot delegate the core strategy of your future business. And that strategy is a digital strategy, not the legacy strategy that built your current empire.

If you can't fire yourself and walk in the next day as the CEO your company needs to survive the digital era, then just fire yourself.

Or eventually, the market will do it for you.

CHAPTER 11:

DIGITAL FOOD CHAIN

ULTURE DOESN'T MATTER.

In chapter 9, we established that Anti-Leaders win all the time. It's true that early cultures most deeply reflect the personalities of their founders. An Anti-Leader is sure to generate an Anti-Culture.

And Anti-Cultures, like Uber's, win. Yes, Kalanick's evil pigeons all came home to roost. But Uber, valued at nearly $70 billion in 2016, has a long way to fall before they hit anything resembling failure. Their private valuation in 2017 was bigger than the market cap of Chrysler, GM, or Ford. And they need to plummet by over 90 percent before they reach their closest competitor, Lyft (valued between $6 billion and $7 billion in 2017).

The market of suppliers (Uber drivers) and buyers (Uber riders) they have built is a powerful engine that cannot easily be disrupted by sensational news and events. It will certainly survive Kalanick's resignation.

So why do so many technology companies, founders, and CEOs keep harping on great culture as one of the secret ingredients for success? Why do legacy chiefs keep focusing on culture as their biggest challenge in digital transformation?

The confusion comes down to a concept we touched on briefly: What Is Most Important When (WIMIW).

WIMIW

I met Bill Campbell a few years before he passed away. Bill is another legend in Silicon Valley, a personal adviser to Apple's Steve Jobs, Google's Larry Page and Sergey Brin, and Twitter and Square's CEO, Jack Dorsey.

Bill believed very strongly that "the world is about great products." He believed that "great products are what's going to drive a company." He went further, adding, "Everything else is a supporting function."

Bill's right. More so in the digital era than ever before in our economic history.

In biology, we're all aware of the food chain.

We sit at the top and eat just about everything. Humans are the apex predator.

But the key to *understanding* the food chain is not to look at the top. It's looking at the bottom. It's looking at how energy flows from one trophic level to the next.

At the base of the food chain, producer organisms such as grasses and plants harvest the abundant energy of the sun, converting it into a massive volume of nutritive substance. Small and large herbivores consume grasses and plants at the next trophic level. Small predators eat small herbivores. Large carnivores eat large herbivores.

And then we eat or kill it all. Each higher trophic level depends completely on the energy provided by the levels below.

Markets are like sunlight. They are a force largely beyond our control. They can only be influenced a little. If a market for your product does not exist or exists in only a limited amount, it does not matter how great a product you build. You will forever be limited by the size of your market.

You can think of the size of your market as the ceiling of the greenhouse in which the seed of your idea will grow. You will grow no higher than your market ceiling (unless you move into adjacent markets).

Which is why product creation is what matters most at the beginning of any startup or digital transformation initiative. In the beginning, don't waste time or energy on anything else.

NUMBERS GAME

The product you create determines the market you enter. It determines the amount of energy you can draw into building your business.

In the digital era, a large percentage of the value of any product will be in its software.

Let's review some basics.

Software is an odd thing to produce. Software is encoded in binary, a method of counting that relies solely on two numbers: 0 and 1.

0 = 0

1 = 1

2 = 10

3 = 11

4 = 100

5 = 101

10 = 1010

Developers start the creation process by writing code in languages such as C and C++, which can be read by humans. Compilers (complex software programs themselves) take these lines of code and turn them into executable binaries—long strings of 0s and 1s that can be interpreted by computer processors, like the ones in your phone.

Any string of 0s and 1s is just a single, big number. So, any software program is just a single, big number.

Once you produce a software program, the marginal cost of production is zero. You can use the same big number for all instances of your product and for all your customers, until your next released version. Microsoft has sold single versions of their releases, such as Windows 4.0 for billions of dollars—trading one number for lots of small numbers that add up to one big number in their bank account.

In the physical world, if you want to make another widget, you need to buy and assemble materials. Materials and assembly add cost.

In the digital world, you can use the same number you already created and just send it or access it over the Internet again.

Even if your product is an iPhone, which has a significant number of sophisticated hardware components, you still benefit from the power of software. Software is what enables you to charge a premium for the piecemeal hardware components you've assembled. Software is a large part of why Apple is such a fantastic cash-generating machine.

Computer processors use operating systems (also complex software) to chop up executable binaries into discrete instructions—for instance, lighting a specific set of pixels on your mobile phone white and another set black, so you can read text on a screen.

Apps are just executable binaries that run on an operating system. They can run on iOS or Android on your phone. Or they can run on Linux or Windows on a server. A number that runs on a number.

Some apps are designed for end users, such as the apps on your iPhone. Other apps sit lower in the stack and talk to each other, such as the wiring and plumbing hidden in the walls of your home. Delphix, for example, is an infrastructure app designed to run on servers or in the cloud.

Apps can be chat bots, voice services, and AI services. Some apps, such as Facebook, Slack, and Trello, become vibrant platforms for other apps.

When apps grow up, they can become Appzillas, powerful forces in the global economy that drive billions of dollars in value and revenues.

The world is an incredible, dynamic canvas, and software paints it in two colors: 0 and 1.

Now that we've established the quirky reality of software, you can begin to see why it changes everything we know about business and economics.

Software has no substance but stores tremendous value.

A single blade of software can be effortlessly turned into an endless sea of grass, limited only by the size of the market—an enormous volume of energy that can be harvested at the next trophic level.

DIGITAL FOOD CHAIN

When you create a product, you decide on a market.

That market may be mature, large, and receptive, in which case, you have an opportunity to quickly build a successful venture (e.g., the Internet when Google emerged). Or that market may be small and limited—for instance, by the availability and cost of bandwidth to the Internet—which will limit you to the rate of growth of the market (e.g., application service providers before Salesforce.com).

Markets are hard or impossible to change, so timing is critical to a new or growing market. But you have a *choice* in the product you create.

Your digital product is the almost-limitless fuel source for your company, bounded only by your market ceiling.

It also sets the reasonable boundaries for your vision.

Your vision sets the boundaries for your mission.

Your vision and mission together set the stage for your culture. Will you be a vision-driven, mission-driven organization of impassioned zealots trying to change the world? Or will you be a gathering of zombies just trying to make it through another week of work?

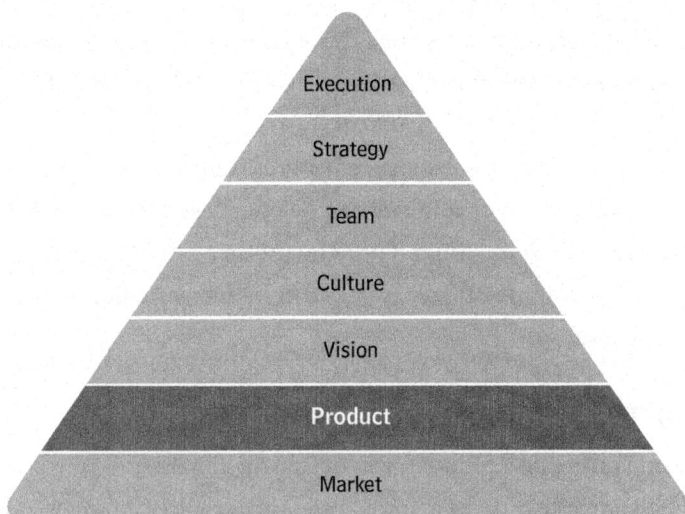

Your culture sets the upper boundary for the team you can assemble, for the quality and type of people you can hire and retain.

The quality of the team you hire will determine the quality of the strategy you can put in place.

Your strategy determines ease, difficulty, and return on execution.

And your execution determines your outcome.

Each trophic level in the Digital Food Chain feeds *and limits* the next.

When people say culture eats strategy for breakfast, they are misunderstanding the underlying framework for success.

Culture doesn't eat strategy. Culture *feeds* strategy. Culture *limits* strategy.

All of which brings us back to the fact that if you have the wrong product, culture doesn't matter.

DIGITAL AVALANCHE

A great product makes everything else easier. It can trigger a Digital Avalanche.

A mediocre product makes everything else harder.

Facebook started with a great product. In a single week, a single individual coded an app that immediately went viral, touching a shared nerve in the human psyche.

Mark Zuckerberg had never been a leader before. He had never hired a team before. He didn't know how to navigate cap tables, term sheets, or equity financings. He didn't have a sense of vision or scale—yet.

But the product determined the vision and mission he *could* set for the company. And it was a big one:

Founded in 2004, Facebook's mission is to give people the power to share and make the world more open and connected. People use Facebook to stay connected with friends and family, to discover what's going on in the world, and to share and express what matters to them.

Viral success triggered an avalanche. Sean Parker came to Zuckerberg and wanted in, and they ousted Zuckerberg's cofounder Eduardo Saverin, setting the stage for an early Anti-Culture.

With Parker's Silicon Valley savvy, they held all the cards when they negotiated their first outside investment from Peter Thiel, cofounder and CEO of PayPal. In addition to Thiel's investment and network, Zuckerberg inherited many of the lessons that made PayPal successful, including Thiel's singular focus on "do one thing." In Facebook's case, the one thing was growth by number of users.

From that point on, the avalanche continued to gather mass, eventually setting a scalable culture and developing Zuckerberg into the civic-minded leader we see today.

As you can see, great products trigger an avalanche of resources and expertise that can propagate through the Digital Food Chain.

You can still set the wrong strategy. Or a competitor can create a better culture, hire a superior team, and catch you with a good-enough or superior product. Or they can outexecute you in go-to-market, sales, and marketing (e.g., VHS versus Betamax).

A great product does not guarantee success. But it can stack the cards in your favor, dramatically altering the odds for success.

As a result, product is what is most important *first*.

CHAPTER 12:
CULTURE

> And it came to pass on the third day, when it
> was morning, that there was thunder and light-
> ning and a thick cloud upon the mount, and
> the voice of a horn exceeding loud, and all the
> people that were in the camp trembled.
>
> —*Exodus 19:16*

I N THE BIBLICAL narrative, Moses ascends Mount Sinai before receiving the Ten Commandments, including thou shalt not kill, thou shalt not steal, and thou shalt not bear false witness.

The Decalogue, as the commandments are known, lays down the most powerful and influential code of culture humankind has ever known. Laws are external. The Decalogue codified a single form of morality that believers actively wanted to internalize, which underpinned the incredible expansion of Western civilization.

Without a code agreed to by all, animal nature prevails, and might makes right. Societies cannot scale. Kingdoms and nations crumble under the weight of chaos and anarchy.

On a MUCH smaller scale, culture plays the same role for companies.

I know what anarchy feels like.

I created it at my first software company, Avamar. I had never hired people or managed a team. I didn't have an experienced founder or CEO to mentor me. I invented a significant, new product and then went about re-creating wheels.

My natural, challenging style ignited discord, especially with sensitive engineers, until I learned my first management principle: (1) Manage yourself. I hired leaders only to find they reduced my leverage and ability to drive execution, which resulted in my next principle: (2) Hire right. I kept leaders and individual contributors too long, when I knew the company could do better, which resulted in my third principle: (3) Fire right.

We raised our first round of venture capital financing in 2000, when the "go big fast" mentality had yet to fully dissipate from the Internet bubble. We immediately started to hire, so we found ourselves in a cavernous, two-story office. We couldn't fill the office with people, so we put ping-pong tables and pool tables upstairs, and we converted the dull, gray cubicles into a specialized football throwing stadium for a game we called Avaball. Players started in the center cubes and moved out with each successful throw into a cube occupied by another player. Miss a throw and you were out. Hurling a football beneath ceiling tiles and above cubicles required an acute side-armed throw.

It was awesome.

But we missed our software deadlines. Not once but tens of times. We ran low on cash and had to do a layoff, more than once. And we had to take a down round.

The only thing that saved us was a great product.

It ensured we had a vision and a mission worth pursuing, worth continued funding, and worth persistent effort. We had invented and eventually shipped a product that would change an industry.

THE PETRI DISH

In the biological world, a culture is a colony of microorganisms that exist, for instance, in a petri dish. For most cultures to flourish, to develop into a strong, growing, and permeating force, they need the right preconditions. Warmth, humidity, and a food supply help cultures grow. Dryness, cold, and starvation can kill a culture.

In the digital world, the product is the starter culture, the vision and mission are the immediate conditions, and capital investment is the food source.

Today, culture must align with the incredible pace of the Innovation Cycle, with the fact that small innovations can explode into massive Appzillas in weeks (e.g., Facebook) or months (e.g., Google).

Facebook, for instance, used to proudly emblazon its walls with one of its cultural tenets: Move Fast and Break Things. If you asked an employee about it, they invariably shared a teaching story—an internal marketing snippet—where a newbie engineer released code that managed to bring down the entire site.

Instead of firing the employee, Facebook kept him and the lesson learned, and the newbie applied himself to developing ways to protect the site from similar failures.

Legacy companies are the opposite.

They do not move fast. They move at a glacial pace. They have an elephant's memory for mistakes and errors. As a result, they develop layers and layers of interdepartmental reviews, checks, and balances—all to safeguard from the many mistakes they have made in the past.

They shift from an offensive to a defensive mindset. Instead of thinking about how to win the market, they think about how not to lose the market.

I've had *Fortune* 500 executives tell me that driving a change in their organization is like pushing a snake. Push in one direction and the snake curls and moves in another direction.

I've had other executives baldly state that "it's good to be king"—that it's good to sit atop a vast multilevel organization and delegate everyday tasks down to countless minions. It can certainly pay well.

Large companies are generally good at producing the ABCs of culture:

- ARROGANCE
- BUREAUCRACY
- COMPLACENCY

But today, small teams can conquer giant empires. Luke Skywalker and Han Solo can marshal a group of rebels, find secret blueprints, and blow apart a Death Star in weeks or months.

Large enterprises might feel safe in their glass-encased high rises with their multibillion-dollar revenue streams, and hundred thousand storm troopers. But they do not appreciate the power of the small company with a product, vision, and mission that sets an impassioned culture of change.

If product, vision, and mission are so important, then how about all the cultural attributes we see marketed by technology companies today?

THE SUCCESS FALLACY

Once a company is successful, everyone wants to imitate that company. Tourists travel every day to Silicon Valley, pouring out of buses to take selfies in front of Facebook's "like" sign. They ooh and aah over Google's wonderland of colors and amenities.

But successful cultures in technology are wildly divergent after you get past great product, vision, and mission. The world is imitating symptoms, not causes.

Both of Google's founders, Larry Page and Sergey Brin, went to Montessori schools and later Stanford. The Googleplex, their headquarters in Mountain View, is a multicolored wonderland, a playground for grown-ups. It's like a graduate extension program that carries the childhood wonder of elementary school over into adulthood.

It's like time stopped for the Google founders when they invented algorithmic search at Stanford, making them modern-day Peter Pans with endless means. But the reality is that 99 percent of their success was preordained the moment they triggered their Digital Avalanche—alone in their garage.

The rest is what success enables them to afford.

Other companies, such as Amazon, eschew Google's perk-heavy approach, building desks out of wooden doors and staying forever frugal.

HubSpot, a marketing automation company, has relentlessly marketed its culture.[25] They call their presentation on culture "part manifesto, part employee handbook, and part diary of our dreams." Not only is it the diary of their dreams, but it also fails to capture the *reality* of their culture.

---

25 slideshare.net/HubSpot/the-hubspot-culture-code-creating-a-company-we-love

I met Dan Lyons, the author of *Disrupted*, over drinks after he published his exposé on the real culture of HubSpot, a revolving door of personnel changes, adolescent misbehavior, binge drinking, and sex in the office.

Once you start studying the cultures of successful technology companies, you come to realize once again that culture doesn't matter.

With the exception of the Anti-Cultures.

ANTI-DIVERSITY STRATEGY

Every successful technology company, without fail, says diversity matters. They substantiate that claim with rationalized self-interest: a more diverse employee base enables a company to hire from the broadest talent pool possible, enabling a company to maintain quality as it scales.

Yet the metrics clearly show a diversity problem in Silicon Valley. Tech companies there are dominated first by young white and then Asian males, especially in the executive and engineering ranks.

If you want to solve a problem, it's important to understand the root cause.

In Peter Thiel's *Zero to One*, he describes the makings of the PayPal Mafia. He admits, "We set out to hire people who would actually enjoy working together. They had to be talented, but even more than that, they had to be excited about working specifically with us."

He goes on to share the philosophy of his cofounder Max Levchin, "Startups should make their early staff as personally similar as possible."

Thiel even shares some quirky details of their mutual interests: "*Cryptonomicon* was required reading, and we preferred the capitalist *Star Wars* to the communist *Star Trek*."

In other words, they purposely employed an Anti-Diversity Strategy, which reduced the friction of divergent cultural backgrounds and ensured the early harmony required to succeed at shipping a great product.

Shipping a great product matters more than anything else.

It helps you win. It helps you scale. And it magnifies your diversity or lack of diversity.

If you ask male venture capitalists over drinks, they'll tell you candidly that they are looking for the prototypical, "blue flame" founding set: two white males in their early twenties, who studied engineering at Stanford and have no girlfriends and no life—other than technology. They are in the blue flame of their careers, their hottest, hardest-working, and brightest burning years.

The formula works. Time and time again. Which is why diversity metrics look so bad across Silicon Valley.

Diversity often becomes an important part of cultures *after* success has been assured, after the lack of diversity has been ingrained in the wood.

To change the diversity equation, you need diversity at the start, not after the fact.

To really fix what's wrong in Silicon Valley, we need diverse founding teams to succeed and become the next wave of Tech Titans and to magnify their diversity based on success.

FAIR WARNING

Another sign of the successful Anti-Culture is a culture of fair warning.

Reed Hasting started the popular trend of publicly sharing internal cultural presentations. The Netflix presentation says, "Real company values are the behaviors and skills that we particularly value in fellow employees." It goes on to say, "Adequate performance gets a generous severance package."

By sharing the cultural manifesto, Hastings, on one hand, is inviting like-minded people to self-select into his organization.

On the other hand, he's giving fair warning to prospective employees: If you sign up, expect the following: "We're a team, not a family.... Netflix leaders hire, develop, and cut smartly so we have stars in every position."

Elon Musk takes it to a further extreme. He likens his companies to joining the elite "special forces" of combat organizations. He borrows the instant image of brutal boot camps for rangers, marines, and Navy SEALs to prepare employees for abusive demands. And still, talented people join.

Jeff Bezos's leadership principle, that leaders "are right a lot," also falls into this category. He's basically saying that employees who join Amazon should expect their leaders to often have all the answers (but remain open to new data), that leaders will often be the "smartest guy in the room." After all, somebody has to be the smartest guy in the room, right?

ORIGIN OF THE CLOUD

OK, I'll admit it. Culture does matter, sometimes. But not for what you think.

In 2002, Bezos issued an internal mandate at Amazon that predestined the cloud. It looked something like this:

1. All teams will henceforth expose their data and functionality through service interfaces.
2. Teams must communicate with each other through these interfaces.

3. There will be no other form of interprocess communication allowed: no direct linking, no direct reads of another team's data store, no shared-memory model, no back doors whatsoever. The only communication allowed is via service interface calls over the network.
4. It doesn't matter what technology they use. HTTP, Corba, Pubsub, custom protocols—doesn't matter. Bezos doesn't care.
5. All service interfaces, without exception, must be designed from the ground up to be externalizable. That is to say, the team must plan and design to be able to expose the interface to developers in the outside world. No exceptions.
6. Anyone who doesn't do this will be fired.

Bezos took an *IT systems architecture* (services-oriented architecture) and applied it to the organization, processes, and culture at Amazon.

It was like a structural explosion inside the company, one that refactored Amazon into a platform company.

Ironically, *Harvard Business Review* published an article a year later, titled "IT Doesn't Matter," by Nicholas Carr, arguing that IT commoditization had already transformed nearly every industry, and the lack of opportunity for differentiation meant companies should be focused on playing defense—risk management and cost containment.

The article was exactly right. And exactly wrong.

Legacy enterprises became incredibly cost conscious, creating layers of decision making and architectural review for every new technology they considered—all in a battle to increase standardization and minimize costs.

In other words, they started to play defense.

But the Bezos mandate changed the world. In 2006, four years later, Amazon's platform transformation gave rise to S3, the simple storage service and the first of Amazon's web services, which we now know collectively as the cloud.

IT can't be compared to the transition from steam engines to railroads or from telegraphs to telephones—technologies that became commoditized utilities that drive little differentiation to businesses today.

IT builds upon itself, each layer of innovation opening new avenues to transform the world.

While the rest of the world played defense, the innovators played offense.

Smartphones proliferated, GPS and mapping matured, and technology companies began to build on the infinite capacity of Amazon's cloud, enabling companies such as Netflix, Airbnb, Spotify, and of course, Amazon itself to break across legacy industries in tidal waves.

In the end, Bezos used a systems architecture to transform his culture, to ship, perhaps, his greatest product of all: the cloud.

CHAPTER 13:

TEAM

N THE AGE of Discovery, Portugal and Spain sent fleets across the unchartered seas to colonize the New World. Cortés and his men arrived in Mexico in the 1500s, during the rule of the Aztec Empire. Not only did they bring superior technology and weapons from a more advanced culture, but they also brought a more advanced disease: smallpox.

While the conquistadors were largely unaffected (their immune systems were more evolved), the deadly virus spread rapidly among the indigenous people, destroying the local population and resulting in the fall of the Aztec Empire.

As we saw earlier, in the Great American Biotic Interchange, animals from the larger and more competitive ecosystem survived where others did not. In the Age of Discovery, the animals were humans.

Today, we've entered a Digital Age of Discovery. Instead of sailing ships across the seas to conquer new lands, technology companies use apps to race instantly across the Internet to stake their claims in industries across the world.

The biological principle still applies: The strongest and most likely to survive evolve in the most competitive ecosystem.

In the digital era, there is no ecosystem as competitive as Silicon Valley.

LOCATION, LOCATION, LOCATION

I grew up in Southern California. With the "success" from Avamar, it took less than a month to raise financing for Delphix. After the close, one of my venture capitalists asked if I really planned on building a second technology company in a "wasteland" like Orange County.

A *wasteland*?

I had spent a fair amount of time in Silicon Valley. It looks nothing like Newport Beach, Laguna Beach, or Corona del Mar, the beautiful beach cities of Orange County. Instead of sprawling land and endless sunshine, you have broken roads meandering aimlessly through dense, old neighborhoods. Modern mansions of the tech elite sit a street away from dilapidated apartment buildings from the 1970s.

If anything, most of Silicon Valley looks like a comparative wasteland, except for the technology ecosystem.

I thought back on my lessons from Avamar. We pioneered an industry-changing technology, but our engineering team shipped product too late. We had a commanding two-year lead, but a Silicon Valley competitor ran us down. We had a hard time finding quality, experienced executives to fill key positions as we scaled and had to settle for those willing to relocate from afar. With an inferior team, we sub optimized product packaging, sales, and marketing.

In the end, we sold for $165 million, and our competitor sold for $2.4 billion.

It didn't take me long to conclude Orange County IS a digital wasteland.

In 2009, we decided to move Delphix to Silicon Valley, where you can buy one-third the house for the same price as what you can buy in Newport Beach (but of course, there's no beach). The high cost of housing compresses disposable income. As a result, homes look a little more worn, cars motor around with dings and dents, and people look a little frumpy and disheveled. I call it the Tech Tax.

Strategically situated in the epicenter of technology, you have the privilege of buying $2 million teardowns on busy streets and the opportunity to gaze wonderingly at roving herds of tech talent.

But that talent can be mighty.

Once I plugged into Silicon Valley's network, I met highly accomplished, articulate engineers who had founded or architected some of the biggest products in enterprise data management.

It's like engineers grew on trees. I picked the talented as quickly as I could.

I had paid the price for weak engineering at Avamar. We didn't just ship product a little late. We shipped product *four years* late. It took several years for us to consume the quality tail—the quality required for a product to reliably support thousands of customers at varying degrees of scale.

In Orange County, there are few, if any, public software companies. We hired the best and brightest engineers we could find at Avamar. Many worked as contractors for the government, building complex software programs like Ada compilers. I later realized that contractors often build themselves *into* their programs. By coding complex, hard-to-support solutions, they guaranteed job security.

That type of contractor-dependent engineering did not work in the world of enterprise software. We needed to ship software that just worked.

As my network widened, I met stronger and stronger engineers and topgraded our team at Delphix. The result? We shipped product by the end of the same year we moved. In December 2009, Staples became our very first customer. And after that, we quickly added big brand name after big brand name.

Engineering quality really matters. So how do you build a strong engineering team?

CROWDING THE HEADPIN

I tell leaders who work for me that I judge them based on their number two. The quality of their top lieutenant tells me if a leader will have the time and leverage to act strategically or if they will be mired in the tactical.

The rule of two is even more important in engineering.

Smart engineers want to work with smart engineers. If you have a persuasive product, vision, and mission in a large market, you can hire talent anywhere, even in Silicon Valley.[26]

At Delphix, I made it my top priority to hire the smartest, most accomplished single engineer I could find. After that, I made it my top priority to crowd the headpin.

In bowling, the headpin sits alone in the first row. The closer you stack the pins to the headpin, the easier it gets to throw a strike. Once we had a critical mass of smart, talented engineers, it became easier and easier to hire while maintaining a high-quality bar.

---

26 If you don't have the magic ingredients, the stronger companies in Silicon Valley will eat you alive.

But if you're not a programmer, how do you identify a strong engineer?

THE LEARNING INTERVIEW

I started Avamar in my early twenties. Since then, I've interviewed thousands and hired hundreds of leaders and individual contributors across the functions required to build a software business—engineering, sales, marketing, finance, support, and so on.

When I first started interviewing, prospects knew far more about their jobs than I did. So, I used interviews to learn about functions and roles.

I'd ask a CMO, for instance, "What makes a great CMO?"

I'd get them to outline their framework for their function. After that, I'd tell them about our capabilities, challenges, and limitations. Then I'd ask them to apply their framework to our situation.

"If you joined, what would your ninety-day plan look like if you had to create it right now?"

If they hemmed or hawed, I'd let out a little pressure and say, "I won't hold you to it, of course. I just want to understand how you think."

After the first candidate outlined an initial framework, I would use it to judge the second candidate's. By the third, fourth, and fifth interview, I had a sophisticated framework to judge any candidate who walked through the door, ranking how they organized the function, prioritized components, and ordered their plans.

I did the same thing with each specific role in engineering.

"What makes a great engineer?"

"How did you architect that product?"

"If you had to build a product like ours, how would you architect it?"

In the end, great engineers ship great products. Not only did we ship product one quarter ahead of plan at Delphix, but we also have some of the highest customer satisfaction and renewal rates in the industry.

SYSTEMS MAP OF SILICON VALLEY

Even *inside* Silicon Valley, location matters.

When we chose the location for our first Delphix headquarters, one of my venture capitalists said to me, "Why don't you put your offices in Redwood City, right next to Oracle's headquarters? You can put up a sign that says, 'Come Join the *Next* Oracle.'"

I wasn't sure if he was joking or not.

To build a data management solution as sophisticated as ours, we needed engineers from some of the top database companies in the world, starting with Oracle. But we also needed great engineers who had solved problems in lower-level systems, such as volume managers and file systems.

As I canvassed the valley, I came to a fascinating conclusion: Silicon Valley is geographically laid out like a systems map.

A basic app systems map looks like this:

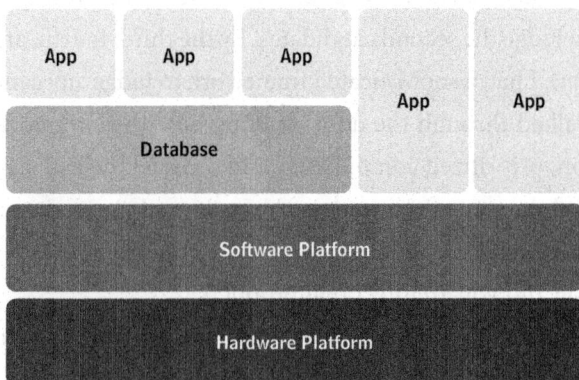

At the bottom, you have hardware platforms, including items such as computer processors, network routers, and storage arrays. As you move up the stack, you have software platforms, such as Apple's Mac OS or iOS operating systems, which mask the complexity of disparate hardware components.

One more level up, you have databases such as Oracle, the data engines that power today's complex applications. And at the top of the stack, you have front-end apps that interact directly with end users, such as enterprise resource planning (ERP) solutions and the apps on your phone.

In the physical world of Silicon Valley, Highway 280 and Route 101 create an artificial island between San Francisco and San Jose. The first hardware giants such as Intel, HP, and Cisco emerged in the South Bay.

As the computer hardware industry matured, it gave rise to the next level in the systems stack: software platforms. As software platforms matured, they gave rise to the next level in the stack: databases. And as databases matured, they gave rise to more and more complex apps. Each layer unlocked the next over time.

San Francisco drew the new layers toward itself like a magnet, which resulted in a funny thing: Silicon Valley laid itself out like a systems map.

Hardware companies such as Intel, Cisco, and Apple sit at the bottom. Software platforms such as VMware, Facebook, and Google sit one layer above them. The world's greatest database company, Oracle, comes next, between San Francisco and the South Bay.

And more and more app companies emerge in San Francisco every day, including Uber, Airbnb, and Twitter.

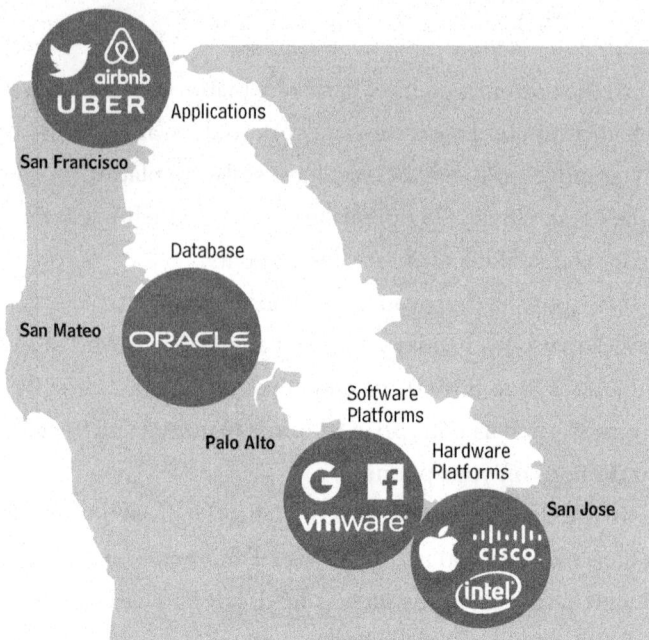

After my analysis, we dropped Delphix in Palo Alto, right between Oracle and the hardware companies. And we drew our engineering and executive talent from both quarters.

Over the last decade, apps have become more and more leveraged, enabling the Ubers and Airbnbs to grow into awesome Appzillas seemingly overnight.

As a result, a major demographic shift has occurred. Talented young engineers want to work where all the hot app companies are headquartered. And they want to live in a big city.

Those twin draws have made San Francisco the new heart of Silicon Valley.

Talent comes first in engineering at Delphix, so we bowed to the laws of the valley and opened a second office in the city.

If you need to hire the world's top technologists, they're probably in the California Bay Area. Just make sure you're looking for them in the exact right place.

BUFFETT INVESTMENT STRATEGY

Warren Buffett has a simple investment strategy: "It's far better to buy a wonderful company at a fair price than a fair company at a wonderful price."

I've learned to apply the same philosophy to hiring.

You can't scale a company by hiring fair (mediocre) executives at a wonderful (cheap) price. You'll need great executives with great experience to maximize your opportunity.

If you have a great product, vision, and mission in a big market, it's easy to build a strong network. If you build a strong network, it's easy to find talent. Once you find the talent, it's easy to hire.

It all starts with great product.

But beware your strengths. Silicon Valley is lined with giant successes. When we began building out our executive team, VMware was the darling of the valley in enterprise software. Our venture capitalists coveted many of their executives, literally calling them "rock stars."

In case you were wondering, digital rock stars look nothing like their musical counterparts.

With product and vision in hand, we added many of VMware's key executives to the team, including VPs in sales, marketing, and product management. They regaled us with detailed stories about their journey and incredible success.

They cost a fortune to hire. And they failed for us.

We thought we bought wonderful executives at a fair price, but we actually bought fair executives at a terrible price.

The Success Fallacy casts an incredible, golden halo on all participants. The key is to see beyond the halo and differentiate between Rocket Builders and Rocket Riders.

ROCKET BUILDERS VERSUS ROCKET RIDERS

In the Western, Judeo-Christian world, we divide the calendar of human history into two phases, BC and AD, or before and after Christ.

In any successful technology company, there are two phases: before the rocket is built (before Product-Market Fit) and after the rocket is built (after PMF). This divides executives and employees into two classes: Rocket Builders and Rocket Riders.

Marissa Mayer is the quintessential example of a Rocket Rider.

I met Mayer briefly at a party. She's shy and unassuming. But she also likes to wear dazzling dresses to chic events such as opening night of the San Francisco Symphony.

Whispers of her achievements trailed all around her at the symphony, back before she took the role as Yahoo's CEO.

Mayer joined Google right out of Stanford as employee number twenty. She directed Google's consumer web products, and she managed the most valuable web page in history: home page for Google search.

When Yahoo's board searched for a new CEO, they understood the power of the Product Trinity and hired for a product CEO.

But they fell for the Success Fallacy. They failed to differentiate between Rocket Riders and Rocket Builders.

In reality, 99 percent of the future success for Google was determined by Larry Page and Sergey Brin working together in their garage.

At the point when they took their first investment from Andreas Bechtolsheim and David Cheriton, they had already achieved PMF.

They launched the Google rocket *from their garage.* Andy and David knew it right away. And they wrote $100,000 checks on the spot.

Mayer didn't do anything wrong. She didn't clutter the home page for search. She didn't add advertisements everywhere. She competently stewarded the site and surely added important innovations in areas such as AdWords.

But evolutionary innovation and significant innovation are two different worlds.

Mayer confidently took the reins at Yahoo. She rifled through the countless projects and searched diligently for the most talented engineers and product managers. She made bold investments and eliminated failing efforts.

But she didn't build a new rocket ship. There would be no salvation. In the end, she sold Yahoo to a legacy telecommunications company for $4.5 billion, collecting $246 million in her failed attempt at saving the once-great Internet giant.

In the digital world, Rocket Riders are legion and Rocket Builders are few.

One of the great ironies is that almost all Rocket Riders honestly *think* they are Rocket Builders. They do the majority of the sustained work, the wide body of execution that makes a company a success. If you interview them, they can tell the detailed story of going from "$100 million to $10 billion" and all the strategies and tactics that were employed.

But all the energy that fueled the body of execution came from the initial creation of the product, vision, and mission, which triggered the Digital Avalanche.

It's what I call the Contribution Paradox.

What Rocket Riders can't tell you is how well they can transfer success and reapply it to a new opportunity, without the supporting history, organization, and system in place around them.

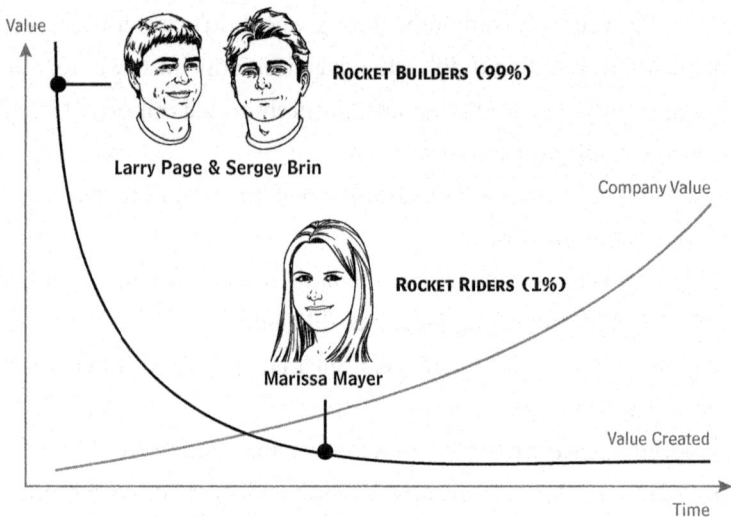

There are exceptions. Sheryl Sandberg, for example, also rode the Google rocket, but unlike Mayer, she decided to pair herself with a Rocket Builder, joining Zuckerberg at Facebook.

For legacy chiefs looking for help from Silicon Valley, beware the Success Fallacy. The only sure Rocket Builders are those who played pivotal, central roles in achieving PMF. And even among Rocket Builders there are one-hit wonders and repeat Rocket Builders.

Of course, Mayer couldn't build a rocket for Yahoo. She never built one at Google.

Larry and Sergey built and launched the rocket long before she joined the company.

CHAPTER 14:
COMPETITION

JYOTI BANSAL GREW up in a small town in India. "I'm obsessed with differentiation," he told me one day.

On the streets of India, competition is fierce. His dad started mom-and-pop shops. At seven years old, Jyoti started going into his dad's shop to help. He watched firsthand the daily struggle to counter the rapidly changing strategies and machinations of competitors. It was literally a matter of life and death for the family business.

Jyoti carried that struggle for differentiation with him when he immigrated to the United States. And it became intrinsic to how he built AppDynamics, the company he founded in 2008.

I shared an office with Jyoti in Silicon Valley when we were first getting our companies off the ground. He always has a twinkle in his eye and a ready smile, so you couldn't see his struggle on the surface. But it was there in every decision he made and in his urgency in building his company.

Jyoti achieved a measure of Zen when he sold his company to Cisco for $3.7 billion on the eve of AppDynamics's planned IPO in 2017, a significantly higher number than the $2.3 billion market cap of their closest competitor, New Relic.

Market caps are the ultimate leaderboard for competition. But it's the hidden struggle *inside* the innovator that defines how we get there.

In the digital world, the ultimate key to competition is the differentiation we build into our products.

CROWDED MARKETS

It's the year 2000.

You're a busy, important venture capitalist. Your opinions really matter, and every dollar in your $500 million fund says so.

A product inventor walks into your office. He tells you he has an incredible product idea. He's decided to build a new, revolutionary MP3 player.

Your interest level plummets. You stifle a yawn and the strong desire to tell him to get out, now. You're trying to be polite and let him finish his thought. You never know if he'll have a better idea you'll want to fund later.

After all, you have one of the new Rios sitting in your computer bag. It has a sleek design, a whizzy display, and a cluster of functions made available by nifty, rounded buttons. You remember picking the Rio from shelves lined with competitive products from Creative, Sony, and companies whose names you didn't recognize and didn't care to remember.

All you know is that the MP3 market is incredibly competitive.

Annoyingly, the inventor gets passionate. He tells you he's going to win the market based on superior *design*.

You've got to be kidding me, you think. Has this guy even seen the incredible range of designs available? How will he compete?

Steve Jobs didn't need to pitch a venture capitalist when he decided to build the iPod. If he had, it might never have been funded. He didn't need approval from anyone.

He had returned to Apple as CEO.

Where others might have seen a crowded market of sophisticated, established competitors, Jobs saw an empty field of sheep. And he was the wolf.

In the words of the wolf:

> There's just a tremendous amount of craftsmanship in between a great idea and a great product. And as you evolve that great idea, it changes and grows. It never comes out like it starts because you learn a lot more as you get into the subtleties of it. And you also find there are tremendous tradeoffs that you have to make. There are just certain things you can't make

electrons do. There are certain things you can't make plastic do. Or glass do. Or factories do. Or robots do.

Designing a product is keeping five thousand things in your brain and fitting them all together in new and different ways to get what you want. And every day you discover something new that is a new problem or a new opportunity to fit these things together a little differently.

And it's that process that is the magic.

When Jobs launched the iPod, he changed the world. It wasn't about music or one thousand songs in your pocket.

He had opened a new dimension in design.

What the world had thought was state of the art in technology design suddenly looked archaic and anachronistic. What had looked like a crowded market suddenly looked stunningly open for a new entrant.

By mastering design, he had changed the nature of digital competition forever.

DECISIONS WITHOUT DATA

Obsessive compulsiveness is a disorder. Perfectionism is a disease.

They stop people from functioning well in normal society. They can destroy relationships and careers. They can be debilitating in almost all phases of life.

But applied to technology products, they can be absolute magic.

Tony Fadell is one of the co-creators of the iPod. He later founded Nest, which was acquired by Alphabet. Over a group dinner and drinks, he shared one of his great beliefs from having worked with product inventors such as Steve Jobs.

"You have to be able to make decisions without data."

In Silicon Valley and in businesses around the world, there's an obsession with data. Data helps us make the right decisions. We need to see the data to act with confidence. Delphix is built on the power of data.

But when it comes to designing products, when it comes to destroying the competition, you need diseases before data. You need perfectionism. You need obsession. You need artistic vision.

Even when building enterprise software products (such as the Dynamic Data Platform at Delphix), I often made hundreds to thousands of product decisions in a week. You collaborate with the members of your team, surface the best ideas, and execute.

At that rate, you can't wait around for all the data. You'll never have the data you need. You need to dial into the magic using an internal compass—one that you've carefully calibrated over time.

Like Jeff Bezos, you can't rely on proxies. Take their input when you can, but ultimately, it comes down to heart, intuition, curiosity, guts, and taste.

I've often likened the product development phase to designing a theoretical dragon.

You start with the core idea—a giant, winged serpent. Then you layer on the features. Impenetrable scales. Razor-sharp talons. A spiked tail. And finally, for user delight, let's let her breathe a raging torrent of fire.

There is no data when you're designing dragons. And if you do it right, there is no competition.

LEVELS OF UXD

Steve Jobs opened the door to a new dimension with the iPod. Then he did it again. And again.

There are multiple levels to designing user experience. At the base, you have Product User Experience Design (UXD), surprising and delighting users with the iPod wheel.

But Jobs didn't stop there.

On top of the product, he layered on Ecosystem UXD. He used iTunes to offload complexity, made the software automatically available on Macs, MacBooks, and later Windows PCs, and negotiated deals with record labels, so customers could easily and legally purchase music.

He moved up one more layer to Company UXD. He integrated Product and Ecosystem UXD with every touchpoint a consumer has with Apple, from messaging, to advertisements, to commercials, to the website. Then he added Apple Stores.

UXD is a multidimensional opportunity in the digital era:

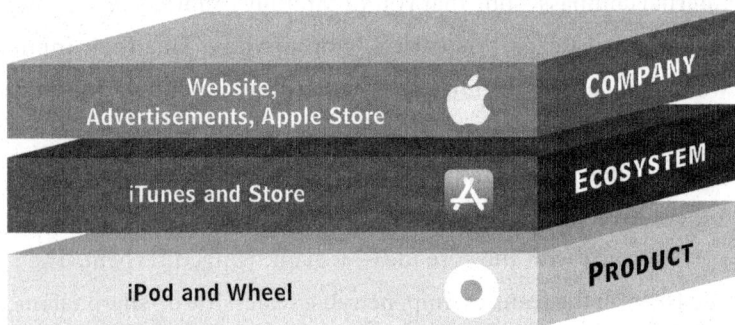

What looked like mastery of UXD with the iPod turned out to be training wheels.

Jobs later applied everything he had learned to building the single greatest technology invention since the Internet: the iPhone. Today, there are more than a billion iPhones in circulation, and Apple will surpass $1 trillion in lifetime sales.

Mastering competition in the digital era requires mastering the three levels of UXD.

CUSTOMER VERSUS USER CENTERED

Jeff Bezos likes to say, "If we can keep our competitors focused on us while we stay focused on the customer, ultimately we'll turn out all right."

Inventors such as Bezos are famous for being great idea machines, building connections, layering on value, and dialing in customer delight everywhere they can.[27]

But "customer centered" doesn't make sense for every company. It can actually *inhibit* growth and company value.

For Google and Facebook, who have a Separation of Users and Buyers, it's really about *user* delight. Their customers—the advertisers—come only after they've built sustained value for their users.

Even in enterprise software, this distinction is important.

Slack sells collaboration software for enterprises. Competitors such as Microsoft Skype and Google Hangouts already have customer relationships with all the enterprises in the world.

Collaboration Software

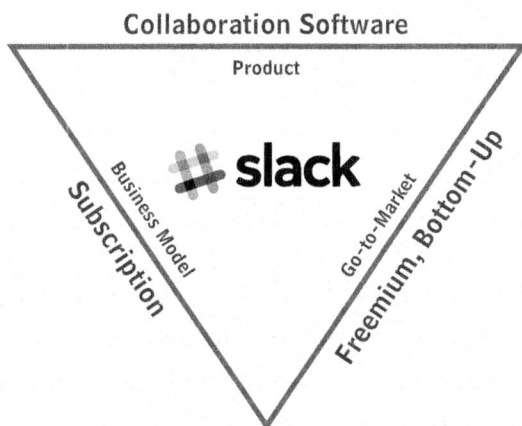

---

27   I have new strategy, marketing, and product ideas all the time and let them compete for my time and attention.

For Slack to compete in the market, they needed to Separate Users and Buyers. They needed to design for users and enable a freemium, bottom-up go-to-market strategy in their product. They needed to design for word-of-mouth-driven virality.

According to Slack's CEO, Stewart Butterfield, "It is especially important for us to build a beautiful, elegant and considerate piece of software. Every bit of grace, refinement, and thoughtfulness on our part will pull people along. Every petty irritation will stop them and give the impression that it is not worth it."

They hired MetaLab, the best UXD consultancy they could find. They dialed in user experience. And it worked.

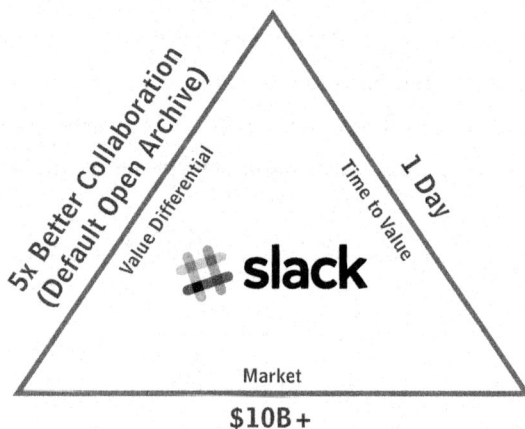

By building their go-to-market strategy into the product and focusing on user design, Slack entered what looked like a crowded market and found plenty of room to grow into an Appzilla.

In the digital era, product design can make competitors disappear ... like magic.

SUMMARY OF PART TWO: THE BUILD

It takes a big vision to attract and retain the talent needed to fuel an Appzilla, and the vision is best preached by a Pied Piper, if you want to build an army of zealots hell-bent on changing the world.

As the Innovation Cycle compresses, the old rules continue to fail. Today, Anti-Leaders and Anti-Cultures often rule their industries, so it takes a pragmatic, prepared mindset to succeed. Leaders need command of the roles that form the Product Trinity (PM, CTO, and UXD), and they need to nurture and focus on the product seeds that will win the future.

What matters most at the beginning is a great product in a large, immediately accessible market. Great products trigger Digital Avalanches that propagate along the Digital Food Chain. Product begets (and limits) vision, which begets culture, which begets team, which begets strategy, which begets execution. The horde of tourists taking selfies at the Facebook "like" sign are falling for the Success Fallacy, worshiping symptoms rather than causes of success.

Many of the most successful technology companies started with Anti-Diversity Strategies (the root of Silicon Valley's diversity problem) and provided Fair Warning to employees about the inhumane hours ahead. Oddly, when systems architectures are applied to organizations and cultures, they can give rise to products, such as Amazon's cloud.

There is no talent pool as deep as Silicon Valley, but even there, location matters, with talent specializing along a systems map that overlays the valley. Learn from the talent you interview to find the best and brightest, then crowd your headpin engineers as closely together as you can. Beware, the valley is filled with Rocket Riders who can tell great tales. But *Rocket Builders* hold the keys.

Finally, do not fear crowded markets if you have mastered the three Levels of UXD (product, ecosystem, and company). You can follow Amazon and center yourself on customers, or better yet, center yourself on users and let customers follow.

PART THREE

THE SCALE

CHAPTER 15:
LOW-GROUND STRATEGY

THE DORDOGNE IN the South of France is one of the most beautiful places on earth. The land is a patchwork quilt of vineyards and fields of lavender. If you speak a little French, the people are warm and welcoming and will share their regional specialties—crispy duck confit and savory cassoulet.

It's also a time machine to the Middle Ages.

Castles sit high on hills to either side of a great, meandering river. Farther in the distance, more castles occupy high-ground perches.

Much of human history has been dominated by a high-ground strategy. In the Middle Ages, if you controlled the high ground, fortifying your castles with armored knights, you controlled the region. In times of peace, the villages in the surrounding area serviced and supported the lords and knights in their castles.

In times of war, the villagers could withdraw into the heavily defended castles. Invading forces had the devil's choice: assail the castle and incur incredibly heavy losses, or try to advance, knowing that castle knights could descend at any time to raid and destroy supply lines, effectively cutting off the ability to feed and provision their armies.

In today's world, however, the low ground is the new high-ground strategy.

As we've seen from companies such as Google, Facebook, and Slack, you start by winning the hearts and minds of the people first. Once you win the people, the castles fall without ever needing to lift a finger.

THE TEACHING SALE

A Low-Ground Strategy isn't available for every product and company. Both Jyoti's AppDynamics and Delphix require traditional enterprise sales forces to assail CIOs in high-ground offices.

Your go-to-market (GTM) strategy defines how you distribute your product to your market of users and customers. This is the typical enterprise GTM Pyramid:

The lower you sell in the pyramid, the more leverage and speed you get in the market. The more complex your product and sale, however, the higher you need to operate in the GTM Pyramid.

Delphix is transformative and complex, because data is transformative and complex.

We help companies reduce software development release cycles from months to daily and intraday releases—over 100x in some cases. We accelerate cloud migrations by 50 percent by eliminating the need to move largely duplicate application environments and enabling faster test and cutover cycles. We also provide real-time data for analytics or AI algorithms.

As a result, our benefits cross multiple functional areas, including development, IT, and business analytics teams, which requires the support of the top-level CIO who owns all these functions. To drive transformation for our customers, we need to educate multiple departments and drive consensus to centralize data provisioning. Then we need to determine which budget categories will fund the program.

It's an intricate, cat-herding sale, but it's worth it.

With all the technology vendors jockeying for a CIO's time, how do you get their attention?

The key is to teach them how to solve a major pain point for their business.

When I met John Chambers, who was Cisco CEO at the time, I asked him about the gating factors to Cisco's growth. John said he woke up each morning and the first thing he looked at was the data coming in about their performance in new international geographies.

At their scale, Cisco could not enable the sale of new products in these geographies without feature updates to their core applications. I explained how fast, secure data delivery into their test environments could accelerate their application release schedules.

Within a few months, we had a high seven-figure sale.

When I met Meg Whitman, HP's CEO, a few months later, I asked her about enterprise releases and their impact on international expansion. Meg shook her head at me. "I'm not interested in application releases. I have to deal with the separation of HP into two companies before I look at anything else."

"You must have hundreds, if not thousands, of applications you need to separate for the two new entities," I pointed out. "You'll need to collect and provision a lot of data to do that successfully."

She stopped and thought about it and told me to email her a summary of what we could do for them.

Within a few months, we had an eight-figure sale.

If you teach customers how to solve a pain point for their business, they will give you the time and attention you need to sell your product. If you solve their pain point, they will become loyal, evangelical customers.

"I'm eternally grateful for our partnership with Delphix."

Scott Spradley
CIO, Hewlett Packard Enterprises

Building a best-in-class enterprise sales force is not for the faint of heart. It takes discipline, insight, and experienced managers and sales reps.

But if your product requires it, it provides a route to market completely within your own control.

RIDING ELEPHANTS

Once upon a time, IBM was the greatest computer company in the world, the two thousand-pound elephant of the technology industry.

IBM built its empire selling mainframe hardware and services.

They decided to employ the same strategy for the once-fledgling PC market. As a result, they decided to outsource development of two key components.

One was the computer processor to Intel. Luckily for Intel, Gordon Moore and Andy Grove had fired themselves from the memory business so they were in a great position to deliver chips for IBM.

The second component was the OS. They outsourced the OS to a young, intense entrepreneur wearing clunky glasses named Bill Gates. He ended up shipping an OS from a little startup he called Microsoft.

What IBM didn't know at the time is that they had just outsourced the single most strategic layer the technology world would see for the next several decades.

Intel and Microsoft rode the IBM elephant into the market, leveraging the second-lowest layer of the GTM Pyramid: the strategic partner.

Ironically, the strategic partner was unstrategic in giving away the keys to the future kingdom.

A few years later, as distributed servers became more and more powerful and filled with more and more Intel chips, IBM found itself with a new problem.

Their hardware had outstripped the needs of the applications in the market. Customers who bought the new servers found they had idle hardware capacity—enormous underutilization of the expensive systems they were buying from IBM.

So IBM inked a deal with a small startup named VMware.

VMware had taken a concept from IBM's mainframe called virtualization, which used software to partition giant hardware boxes into smaller units of operation. By virtualizing these new, high-powered servers, VMware could carve a single server into a series of "virtual machines." The applications and OSs that run in virtual machines *think* they are running on their own physical hardware, but they're really running in software apartments.

In 2017, VMware's $7 billion in annual sales support a market cap over $37 billion.

If you can catch a ride on an elephant, it can be the fastest path to market domination. If you're an innovator in a large enterprise, the elephant might be your parent company—an incredible advantage.

Luckily for companies like Intel, Microsoft, and VMware, IBM has been happy to oblige, over and over and over again.

DEATH OF A SALESMAN

Chinese use the phrase, "the frog in the well," to describe a narrow-minded person. A frog, living at the bottom of a well, sees only a narrow circle of sky. It has no view of the vast world beyond the constraints of the well.

In the digital era, it can pay to be the frog in the well.

Atlassian's founders started their company in Australia, making developer tools. They took advantage of an incredible Value Seam that opened in the market.

For decades, enterprises developed software in large, master-planned "waterfall" programs that could take years to develop, with requirements flowing down from architecture and design, to development, quality assurance, and a final release.

The waterfall method required lengthy analysis and central-ized planning. By the time all the software finally made it through the lengthy phases, the world had often changed and the require-ments no longer met market needs.

A colossal waste of time, money, and effort.

Agile development emerged as a new and superior method for most software programs. Small teams of developers, product managers, and testing engineers work together to release useful software in fast, discrete increments, often in as little as two-week sprints.

Waterfall to agile is another example of centralization and decentralization cycles.[28]

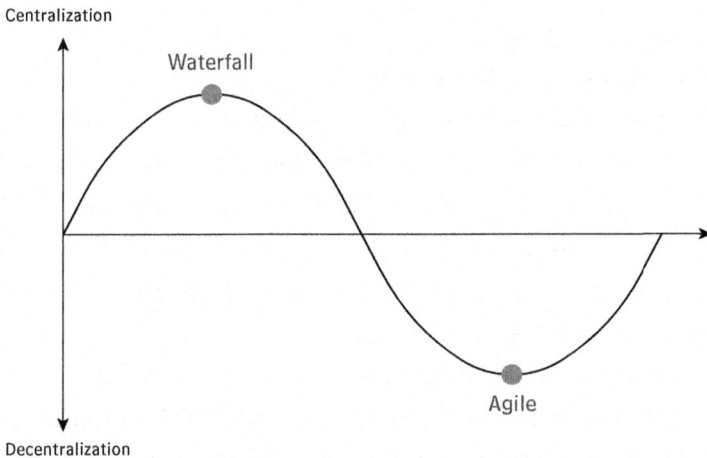

Centralization

Waterfall

Agile

Decentralization

---

28 Application architectures have followed a similar cycle, moving from centralized "monolithic" apps to decentralized apps made from a multitude of microservices. There's evidence of the cycle returning to centralization with the large-scale ser-vices or "mega-services" now available in clouds that can be easily employed by app vendors.

The tools developed to manage waterfall engineering were too heavyweight and slow to match the pace of Agile development, but Atlassian was small and nimble. So they adapted their tools and messaging to fill the emerging Value Seam.

Their founders knew a lot about development, but they didn't know anything about selling enterprise software.

They did something highly unusual in the world of enterprise software: they put their software up for sale on the Internet and refused to hire salespeople.

And companies around the world bought their products online.

In 2017, Atlassian generates nearly half a billion dollars a year in revenue with a market cap greater than $8 billion. According to Scott Farquhar, Atlassian co-CEO, "Customers don't want to call a salesperson if they don't have to. They'd much rather be able to find the answers on the website."

Critics such as Peter Levine, a partner at venture capital firm Andreessen Horowitz, have pointed out that a direct enterprise sales force could accelerate the adoption of Atlassian products and revenue growth. Instead of trusting the products to sell themselves over the Internet, use highly trained salespeople to drive awareness, adoption, and advocacy.

But Peter's missing the point.

He doesn't understand the incredible power of the frog in the well. Atlassian built their products for the five hundred thousand businesses worldwide that can use their software, not for the five thousand biggest enterprises that expect to be sold to by enterprise salespeople.

By focusing on their narrow window to the world, the Internet browser, they have mastered a fully digital GTM strategy, one that lets them sell to the world, salespeople-free.

If they had started to hire enterprise salespeople early on, they would have divided their efforts and perhaps failed at both or become too reliant on the enterprise model, narrowing in for the few instead of servicing the many.

Instead, they persisted with their Low-Ground Strategy, and they ended up building one of the fastest-growing enterprise software companies in the world today.

For the modern innovator, build a Low-Ground Strategy into your product if you can, so you can tap into the power of the frog in the well. In the end, the window of the Internet may be the best window of all.

CHAPTER 16:
THE MARKETING RABBIT HOLE

Alice started to her feet, for it flashed across her mind that she
had never before seen a rabbit with either a waistcoat-pocket,
or a watch to take out of it, and burning with curiosity, she
ran across the field after it, and fortunately was just in time to
see it pop down a large rabbit-hole under the hedge.
In another moment down went Alice after it, never once
considering how in the world she was to get out again.
—Lewis Carroll, *Alice's Adventures in Wonderland*

ATLASSIAN'S DIGITAL SALES would never have converted
half a billion dollars a year in sales over the Internet
without a digital marketing strategy.

But beware chasing the rabbit down the hole—you
may never look at marketing the same again.

Today, digital marketing has taken Silicon Valley
by storm. If you go down the rabbit hole, you will meet strange
and interesting characters you have never heard of or seen before.

For decades, CMOs have kept famous John Wanamaker's
quote from the turn of the twentieth century: "Half the money
I spend on advertising is wasted; the trouble is I don't know
which half."

That's no longer true. Today, you can see attribution data for nearly all your marketing if you execute a Low-Ground Strategy.

In classic high-ground strategy, your PR firm targets media, analysts, and influencers with your brand, category, and messaging to drive awareness of your company and products. You can take advantage of this "air cover" by pairing it with demand-generation programs: events, webinars, partner marketing, field marketing, and digital strategies to create a pipeline of opportunities for your sales reps to convert. You feed these programs with content from product marketing that populates your website, blogs, data sheets, and white papers.

You organize the efforts in a series of campaigns with unified themes and watch as the pipeline builds and turns into sales dollars (or not).

But companies like Atlassian didn't spend money on PR or even search advertising early in their development. They built their empire on the most powerful marketing today: digital word of mouth.

STORYTELLING

Great high- and low-ground marketing both start in the same place: storytelling.

Humans have evolved to naturally learn from stories or narratives. We love to hear stories, and we love to tell stories.

The best stories propagate naturally, passed on from one human being to another. With the rise of social media and networks, stories pass from one to many and from many to many more in a matter of *seconds*.

To tell a crisp, compelling story about a company, you start with the core messaging. Newspapers have long trained reporters to ask the six key questions in an interview: who, what, where, why, when, and how?

In the digital era, you have less time to tell stories because markets are overcrowded with competing stories. And you need to tell a consistent story across all content and channels, or your story will never propagate. So it's important to narrow the message down to the three most important questions.

You can break down the core elements of a story with a messaging framework, answering "who, what, and why," with three supporting pillars for each question.[29] Here's an example, using the Delphix story:

WHO: MISSION TO LIBERATE DATA, ACCELERATE INNOVATION		
Data Volume, Demands Exploding	Data Trapped in Silos	Data Friction Slows Innovation

WHAT: DYNAMIC DATA PLATFORM		
Fast, Secure Access	Self-Service Data Pods	Everywhere: On-Premises, Multi Cloud

WHY: FAST EAT THE SLOW		
Data Speed Changes Everything	DataOps: People, Process, Tech	Turn Data Into Action

Core messages provide an underlying skeleton to unify all content. Here's an example of messaging based on the skeleton above:

At Delphix, our mission is to liberate data and help companies accelerate innovation.

---

29 This messaging framework is inspired by conversations with David McJannet, CEO of HashiCorp, and Marc Holmes, VP Product & Revenue Marketing at Chef.

Today, companies need to satisfy a range of data demands to accelerate app development, to migrate apps to the cloud, and to leverage analytics and AI.

But data continues to grow in silos, in hundreds to thousands of applications, all closely guarded by centralized IT organizations. Data friction slows everything. As data gets larger and more complex, it gets harder to move.

Delphix provides the first Dynamic Data Platform to provide fast, secure access to data, breaking data free of application silos. Instead of heavyweight data closely guarded by centralized IT, Delphix has invented weightless self-service Data Pods.

Data Pods transform the economics and physics of data. Data Pods use pointers instead of physical copies to virtualize data across dev, test, QA, training, and analytics environments and can move data everywhere—across datacenters or clouds.

In the digital era, the fast eat the slow. Data speed changes everything. It enables the practice of DataOps, the alignment of people, process, and technology to optimize the flow of data. With Delphix businesses can liberally use data for all their needs, turning data into action, so they can win in the digital era.

Marketing teams can take a core-messaging framework and create a range of content, testing messages with audiences and iterating into the most persuasive story they can tell.

CATEGORY CREATION

I learned about the importance of category at my first software company. In the early years at Avamar, we struggled through missionary sales, even though we had a significant value differential.

We could store a full backup on disk in less than 1 percent of what it took on tape, and we could restore data 50 percent faster.

The competitors who followed us into the market struggled as well. We all called our solutions something different—a zebra, a donkey, a pony. We hired highly successful, skilled sales reps from tape software vendors, and they struggled, too.

One day, at a storage conference, an analyst got on stage and began describing the wave of new entrants in the data backup space, using all our varied descriptions. Midway through, he became frustrated and declared, "Enough with all these descriptions. You're all data deduplication companies. It's dedupe."

The analyst named the horse. As all the competing vendors fell in line with the category name, it generated momentum in the market. Suddenly, all our individual marketing budgets and programs coalesced into a single wave, educating customers worldwide.

Instead of going from customer to customer, evangelizing the benefits of backing up data to disk for the first time, customers began calling us, asking how we differentiated from other data dedupe solutions.

As a result, salespeople who struggled to close $1 million a year in sales suddenly went flush, closing $5 million a year.

The product hadn't changed. The competitive landscape hadn't changed. The market hadn't grown. But sales started pouring in.

Categories carve out a space in the buyer's mind.

A great category will carve out its space quickly and then enable the category to propagate, from one customer to many.

For Delphix, our category is DataOps. Instead of having admins centrally administer and provision data from system to system, creating redundant, heavyweight, and expensive copies everywhere, we automate and streamline all the data with our DataOps platform.

Delphix decentralizes access and control over data, enabling a cycle of its own:

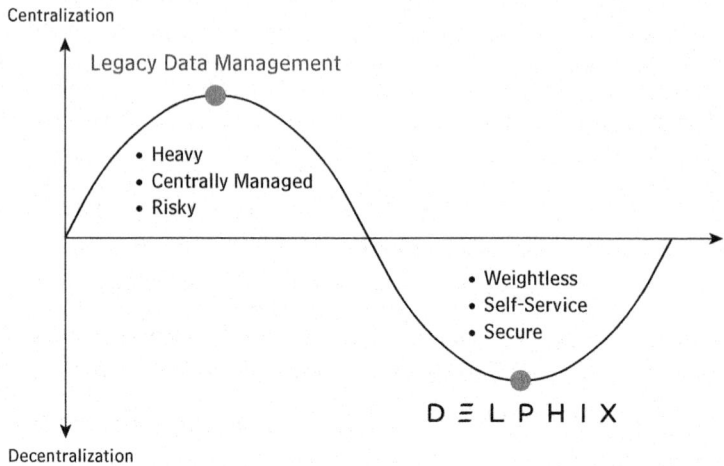

Centralization

Legacy Data Management

- Heavy
- Centrally Managed
- Risky

- Weightless
- Self-Service
- Secure

D Ξ L P H I X

Decentralization

CATEGORY-FREE

Down in the marketing rabbit hole, categories don't matter.

Atlassian, for instance, still doesn't have a natural category. They do everything they can to avoid the category "developer tools," an unstrategic category filled with legacy vendors with middling or no growth that would actually damage their revenue multiples and market cap.

The category "collaboration tools" or "collaboration software," however, is hardly better, because it instantly brings to mind solutions such as Google Apps, Microsoft SharePoint, and even communications tools such as Slack and Skype.

It's the Goldilocks dilemma: One bed is too small. The other is too big.

Luckily, they employ a Low-Ground Strategy, where user experience and digital word of mouth trump abstract marketing.

Atlassian has spent years defining and refining an Internet communications strategy targeting very specific types of individuals called personas.

On Atlassian's website, they used to share details of their personas, which included a picture, gender, specific age, title, description, and quotes to indicate motivations and emotions. They used data from countless interviews and research to build these personas— highly tuned representations of customer types.

In the digital era, you use personas to design everything from products and interfaces, to customer journeys, to websites and marketing content. You can digitally plan persona journeys from discover, to try, to buy, to advocate—and then watch the data to see how many move from one phase to the next.

Personas help you build empathy for your users and customers. They help you feel what your customers feel.

It turns out developers *hate* marketing. They *hate* being sold. They don't care about high-level categories. They want specific tools for specific purposes, such as issue trackers. And they love products they can access over the Internet and test on their own.

So Atlassian sold it to them that way, through the window of the Internet.

TWEEDLE A AND TWEEDLE B

Articulate, stylish, and savvy leaders have long led marketing.

Not anymore. Developers run the new broadcast towers.

Today, in Silicon Valley many of the most successful marketing executives have a development background and hire technologists as marketing operations leaders. As marketing tools continue to proliferate and developer versions of everything emerge, technically competent marketing teams will disproportionately win.[30]

A few decades ago, the most powerful, wealthy businesses consumed most of the television and print ads and paid for time with the biggest analysts and influencers—a concentrated, tightly controlled funnel to reach the widest audience.

Today, billions of people Google the Internet for what *they* want to buy, not what vendors want to sell. The Internet inverts the funnel, letting customers click through search results to self-educate and self-select.

Instead of a small number of highly selective influencers, social media and online review sites have completely democratized influence. Today, anyone can attract a following on Twitter and influence all their friends with a post on Facebook.

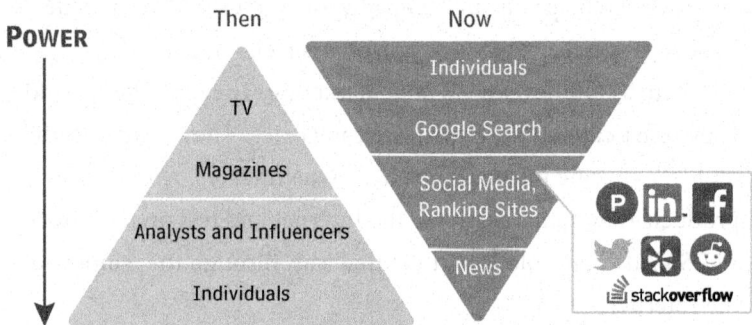

---

30   Both David McJannet and Marc Holmes are examples of marketing leaders with backgrounds in software development. Having held leadership roles at VMware and Hortonworks (public big data company), David has been keenly focused on the power of digital marketing to create market categories and engage users at scale, and of course, HashiCorp lives and breathes digital marketing today.

The democratization of influence has produced hundreds of startups in marketing, all busily carving out their niches and refactoring the industry.

Just a few years ago, companies such as Eloqua, Marketo, and HubSpot crested on the wave of marketing automation.

But their centralized empires have already been deconstructed by the next wave of developer-centric tools:

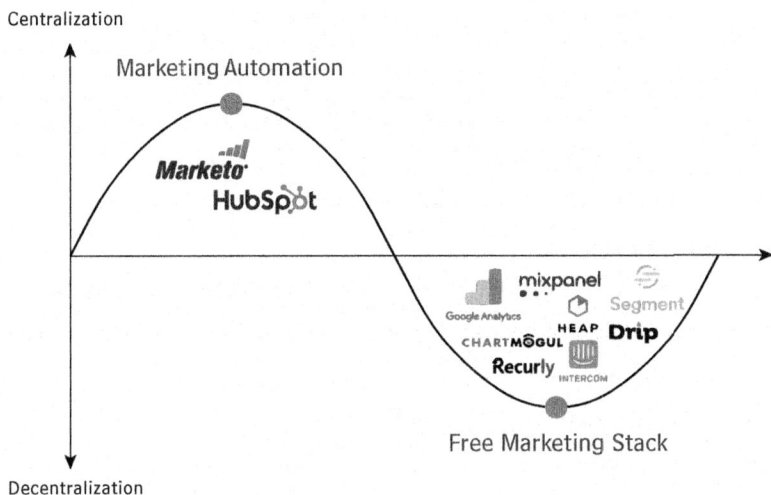

Today, you can build a sophisticated, flexible marketing stack that rivals or supersedes what the world's largest companies can buy with their millions of dollars in marketing budgets—for free.

For instance, you can analyze your funnel, track cohorts, and track all your website visitors and events with Segment, Mixpanel, and Google Analytics. You can track every click, tap, and gesture from users of your app with Heap.

You can run A/B tests on your website or email campaigns, capture leads, create drip email campaigns, and set up workflows with Drip. You can respond to, engage with, and support customers in real time with Intercom. And you can bill your customers and see your subscription analytics with Recurly and ChartMogul.

You can feed this technical marketing stack with search engine optimization (SEO), paid search, and social media marketing—all while staying within the digital window of the Internet.

By mastering personas and empathy, focusing on user or customer experience and journeys, and religiously testing different options (A test versus B test or A/B testing), innovators can harness the power of a digital marketing stack to scale their companies cost effectively, all while staying largely under the radar.

Unless you've been to Wonderland, these companies and categories sound new and unfamiliar, but the most successful of these will become as iconic as the Cheshire Cat, the Mad Hatter, and the March Hare.

Companies that master the Low-Ground Strategy in marketing have a growing economic advantage over those still trapped in the last era.

It's time to disrupt marketing or die.

CHAPTER 17:
EXECUTION

New York Yankees
$114,457,768
vs
$39,722,689
Oakland Athletics
—Opening frame of critically
acclaimed movie *Moneyball*

N THE MOVIE *Moneyball*, the Oakland As make the 2002 play-offs despite fielding a team payroll one-third the size of the highest-paid team, the New York Yankees. The secret in this David and Goliath story comes down to hidden, underlying metrics discovered by the Oakland As.

Rather than emphasize batting averages and stolen bases, the As focused on better, overlooked indicators for success: on-base and slugging percentages.

It's easy to learn the wrong lessons from big, dramatic successes. Companies such as Uber have consumed tens of billions of dollars and still hemorrhage billions a year to amass their $70 billion market caps. Amazon reported vast losses for twenty years, while investors continued to support Bezos's growth strategy. Facebook refused to sell advertising while amassing millions a year in computing expenses to ensure continued user growth.

Reid Hoffman, a partner at Greylock and chairman and founder of LinkedIn, calls it blitzscaling: "It's the science and art of rapidly building out a company to serve a large and usually global market, with the goal of becoming the first mover at scale."

Very few companies can blitzscale successfully. They are the companies that have already triggered the Digital Avalanche and are harvesting the incredible energy being created by accelerating momentum.

There's also danger in the narrative. Blitzscaling feeds the Success Fallacy. We all know and remember the successes. But how many companies have blitzscaled and failed?[31]

PAY TO GROW

Blitzscaling sits at the divergence of interests between venture capitalists (VCs) and entrepreneurs.

All things being equal, a VC would prefer a company to consume more capital to reach the same market cap. Let's imagine two outcomes: (A) Startup A consumes $20 million to build a $1 billion exit, netting the VCs 20 percent or $200 million; or (B) Startup B consumes $100 million to build a $1 billion exit, netting the VCs 51 percent or $501 million.

VCs want scenario B. With superfunds (>$1 billion) aplenty these days, VCs need to put a lot of capital to work to appease their investors and justify high management fees (2 percent per year

---

31   You can also attribute this to survivorship bias.

standard). Twenty million dollars is a big management fee for ten partners to consume *before* generating any returns.

The highest returns for VCs come from early rounds (Series Seed, A, and B), but the safest places to put large amounts to work are big, later rounds, especially when the VCs already have a clear view on how well a company is performing.

Every round of investment a startup takes typically puts more shares and more control into VC hands. In scenario B, VCs tip over 51 percent—full shareholder control if they have preferred terms.

If you run a successful startup, it can feel like the VCs want to force-feed you capital like a goose. We all know the result: foie gras.

There's a difference between VCs and founders. Founders bleed their companies. They generally have the longest-term view at heart. They are like parents. They care for their children for their *entire* lives.

VCs, however, will typically exit shortly after an IPO—they are looking for a return within a targeted time frame. They want the maximum valuation and ownership over their period of investment.

Blitzscaling can accomplish that objective (if not blitzscaling, then its evil VC twin, blitzfeeding).

But what happens to the companies?

Building great companies requires discipline and operational excellence. A culture of frugality helps maximize return on capital. And the value of capital efficiency is highest during the inevitable dark days.

A company that blitzscales and fails to convert spending into long-term value can be thrown into chaos, its culture irreparably reset with a grow-at-any-cost mentality. That can help fatten up a calf before the kill, but it's not great for long-term health.

Companies such as GitHub started out lean and became cash-flow positive early but then consumed vast amounts of capital and began blitzscaling. The results: an organization in turmoil, an ousted founding CEO, a surge in layers of management, a flood of key executive and technical departures, and a layoff.

Companies such as SoundCloud, Medium, and Twitter have all paid to grow, adding tremendous weight to their vessels that their revenue and business models cannot float, leaving their futures in jeopardy.

Instead of throwing lavish parties, startups should look at funding events as necessary evils, an increase in their mortgage they will surely pay back with interest. And innovators inside of large enterprises should be equally mindful of capital efficiency.[32]

Did these companies need to blitzscale to reach critical mass in network size to outgrow competitors? Could they have scaled as rapidly or close to as rapidly with more financial discipline?

Unfortunately, once you blitzscale, the effects are often petrified into the company's cultural wood.

SALES BEFORE EXPENSE

Atlassian reached an $8 billion market cap by minding the rule of law for every mom-and-pop shop around the world: Sales Before Expense.

If you spend money faster than you can bring money in from sales, you die. It's that simple.

They accepted a small round of investment from a Silicon

---

32 Innovation within a large enterprise is less likely to encounter pressure to blitzscale and consume large amounts of capital. Instead, the reverse may be more likely: difficulty convincing the parent company to invest sufficiently off the balance sheet and fear of impacting quarterly operating margins.

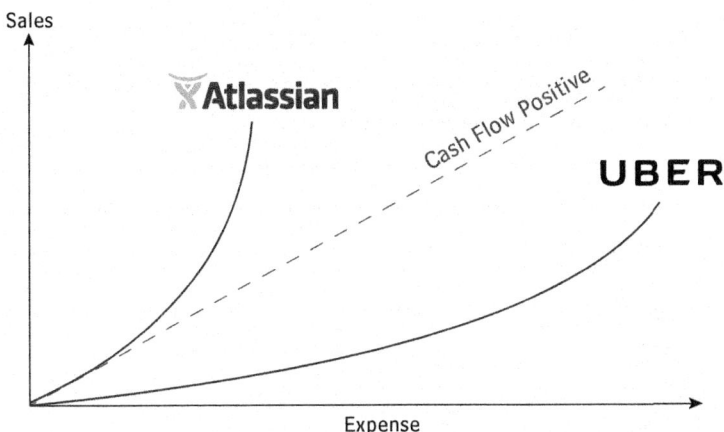

Valley VC firm, but they didn't use a cent of the investment to grow their business. Instead, most of the investment went right to employees who wanted a little liquidity (e.g., to buy homes, put kids through college, pay down debt, etc.) five years prior to the IPO.

What about the increased cost to break even in today's digital world?

Let's take enterprise software-as-a-service (SaaS) companies as an example. They often provide freemium offerings to get started and need to pay for infrastructure or cloud expenses up front. In addition, with a subscription sales model, where companies pay by the drink, they get small dollars up front compared to legacy perpetual-license models.

For instance, instead of collecting $100,000 up front for a perpetual license along with $20,000 in first-year maintenance, SaaS companies collect $5,000 a month, or $60,000 a year. As a result, it takes them more than two years to collect the same amount in sales.[33] They get less money up front to cover expenses *and* more expenses, because they include the hardware and management of the software in the service.

As a result, SaaS companies often need to reach $100 million in annual recurring revenues before they reach a scale that enables them to break even.

Perpetual (License + Maintenance)   **Subscription**

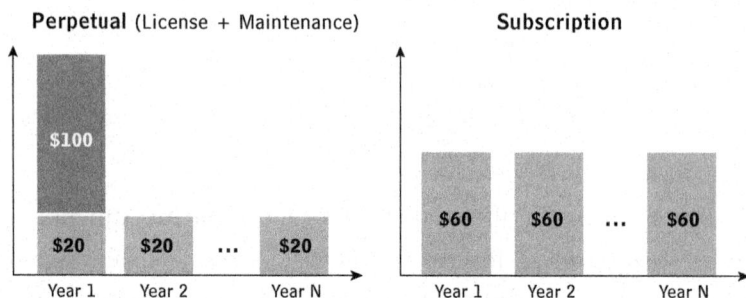

This is where business models and execution play important roles.

At Delphix, we decided to sell software in the cloud or on-premises under a subscription license model. By selling software instead of SaaS, we didn't need to carry the infrastructure or cloud expenses, even when we offered free trials.

In addition, instead of asking for monthly or annual payments, we asked customers to pay for three years in advance. Of course, we also offered them the ability to pay in shorter increments of one or two years in advance, but many of our customers were happy to pay for three-year subscriptions.

By implementing a hybrid business model (selling software on only a subscription model) and asking for multiyear payments up

---

33   After two years, however, SaaS models generate a higher customer lifetime annuity than the typical 20 percent maintenance streams from perpetual software license sales.

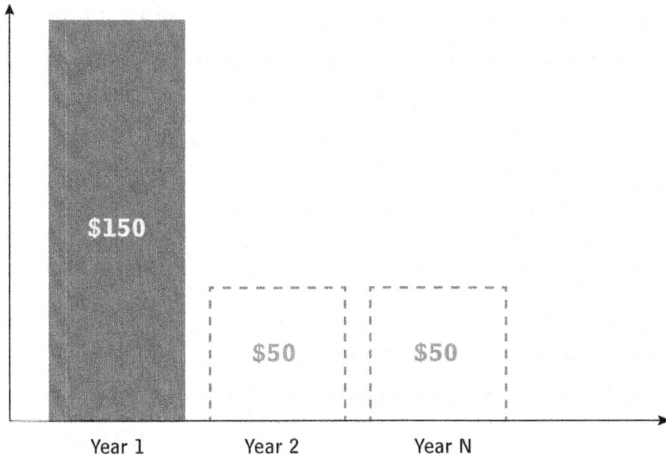

3Y Up-Front Subscription

front, we had the best of both worlds. In the words of our customer SAB Miller (makers of Miller Lite), we have a business model that both "tastes great" and is "less filling."

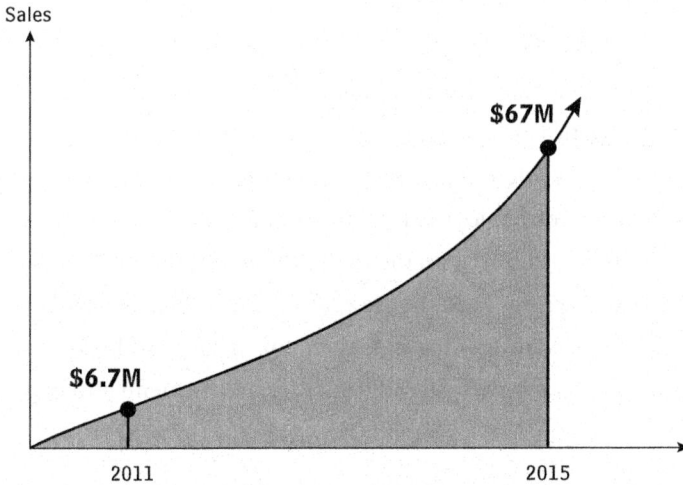

In my last four years as CEO and before transitioning to a chairman role, we grew 1,000 percent, from $6.7 million to $67 million and *added* a few million in cash in the bank from generating more sales and cash flow than we spent.

We generated $200 million in cumulative sales, while consuming a total of only $15 million in VC dollars (we raised more but left it in the bank). To put that into perspective, a typical legacy implementation of an enterprise resource planning (ERP) solution (just getting a prepackaged piece of software to run for a customer) costs around the same $15 million.

That's all it took to build an enterprise software company that received $1 billion term sheets in our last round in 2015.[34]

In the end, you never want to constrain the growth of a healthy business by underspending if you have ready access to capital. But overspending can have disastrous long-term consequences, so beware the call to blitzscale.

GROWTH FRAMEWORKS

Frameworks can help you learn. They can also help you scale.

At PayPal and LinkedIn, Reid Hoffman applied frameworks and heuristics everywhere to help his companies scale.

Reid gave me an example from daily life—a simple framework to increase your enjoyment of meals in restaurants.

If he finds himself on the road in an unfamiliar restaurant, he orders defensively. He'll choose a safe option with a high likelihood of decent execution—roast chicken, for instance. If he knows it's a quality restaurant, he'll range further on the menu and explore,

---

34 We decided to go with the highest quality investor and terms rather than the highest valuation, so the final valuation was under $1 billion.

ordering riskier items, such as clam and mussel linguine.

Explicit, written frameworks and heuristics help teams make decisions quickly and forge alignment. Often, when teams disagree and can't resolve arguments, disparate underlying frameworks are the problem. If you surface, debate, and agree on the framework, everyone can fall into alignment.

Frameworks make it easy for teams to disagree and commit.[35]

There are several metaframeworks or management methodologies in Silicon Valley that have helped companies scale.

At Cisco, John Chambers used a system he called VSE or vision, strategy, and execution. At Salesforce.com, Marc Benioff uses a system he calls V2MOM, which stands for vision, values, methods, obstacles, and measures. Peter Thiel used the "one thing" approach at PayPal.

I prefer OKRs, or objectives and key results.

John Doerr is another Silicon Valley legend. He's backed even more legendary entrepreneurs, including Google's Larry Page and Sergey Brin, Amazon's Jeff Bezos, and Twitter's Jack Dorsey.

John hosted a breakfast to discuss OKRs. He learned about OKRs in the 1970s when he worked at Intel. After firing himself, Andy Grove and the management team created OKRs to help Intel transition from a memory to a microprocessor company.

When John later introduced the concept to Google, Larry and Sergey immediately saw the value and embraced it. OKRs helped Intel scale into a computer hardware juggernaut that has lasted through the ages. And it helped Google scale from forty to forty thousand employees.

OKRs enable collaboration, alignment, focus, and accountability

---

35   Disagree and commit is another one of Bezos's leadership principles.

throughout a company. All employees are encouraged to create and publicly share OKRs that align all the way up to the CEO.

In general, each individual should have three objectives that are qualitative and inspirational, focusing on what matters most. These objectives are purposely limited, so they are not supposed to be comprehensive.

Each objective should be measurable by three key results, with a numerical grade that can be measured for a defined period, such as a quarter. Google uses a system from 0 to 1 (e.g., 0, .5, 1).

Key results should be set as stretch goals, so they should not be easy or impossible. If you set them right, key results should only be achieved at a 70 percent rate.

At companies such as Google, OKRs are discussed frequently and transparently across the company, with formal grades each quarter and then a quarterly reset.

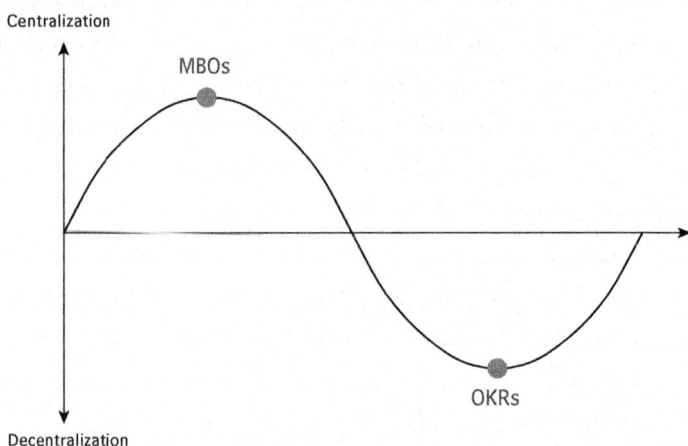

In the cycles of management methodologies, OKRs are the faster, decentralized versions of centralized legacy methods such as MBOs, or management by objectives. Instead of infrequent, annual reviews of MBOs in confidential conversations between an employee and a manager to determine compensation, OKRs are far more frequent, publicly shared, and focused on operational efficiency.

OKRs are a proven framework for scaling technology companies. There are also a host of startups that have built apps for OKRs, including Betterworks, Perdoo, Weekdone, Atiim, Statuspath, and 7Geese.

But what about the actual metrics you need to scale your idea as fast as possible, the content inside the OKRs?

What's the digital equivalent of on-base and slugging percentage—*Moneyball* for the digital era?

MAGIC METRICS

On its meteoric rise to two billion users, Facebook collected a lot of data.

They collected logins, friend requests, clicks, usage duration, page views, search entries—everything you can imagine. They ran trials, experiments, and A/B tests. They generated an enormous range of complex data. They were data rich and insight poor.

Until they divined their Magic Metric.

Chamath Palihapitiya, now a VC, but at the time a coder who headed up the growth team at Facebook, finally had an aha moment when he distilled all the data down to a single actionable metric: seven friends in ten days.

If a Facebook user added seven friends in ten days, they were likely a user for life.

That simple metric, distilled from all the noise, became the North Star for the entire organization. They did everything they could to get a user to add seven friends in ten days. That metric helped them separate retained from churned users, so they could increase retention and reduce churn.

At Twitter, they wanted users to follow thirty people. At Zynga, they wanted users to come back the next day after signing up, what they called "day one retention." At Slack, they wanted teams to send two thousand messages. At Delphix, we want customers to launch five Data Pods for each instance of the software.

You'll know you've identified your *Moneyball* metric when you can ride it to scale.

After identifying their Magic Metric, Facebook knew they would win even when they had 45 million users and MySpace had 115 million. According to Palihapitiya, "We just knew it.... We knew what we were doing."

Divining a Magic Metric can enable the terrifying growth that results in industry-eating Appzillas, so find yours as fast as you can.

CHAPTER 18:

PLANET OF THE APES

N 1883, THE earth bore witness to one of the most catastrophic explosions in modern history. It wiped out the entire ecosystem of living organisms on an island in Indonesia called Krakatoa.

It began with a volcanic eruption. Scorching-hot lava collided with cold seawater.

The result? Water flash-boiled into a cloud of superheated steam estimated at ten thousand times the force of Hiroshima—a phreatomagmatic event.

The aftermath fascinated a generation of evolutionary biologists, including E. O. Wilson, one of my favorite professors in college. Wilson spoke reverently of the unique opportunity to watch the powerful forces of evolution play out on a slate wiped clean—creating a survival dynamic where colonizing species of flora and fauna battled for supremacy across niches within a pristine ecosystem.

Amazon's cloud is a digital phreatomagmatic event in reverse.

First it created a clean slate for an ecosystem of apps to flourish and compete. Now it's in the process of flash-boiling apps across a vast array of legacy ecosystems, including the ecosystems themselves.

But let's start at Amazon's beginning.

NESTING DOLLS

For more than a century, Russians have been crafting wooden nesting dolls, or *matryoshka* dolls, shaped like a little matronly woman wearing a sarafan dress. Open her up, and you find a smaller version inside. Open the second, and you find another, and another, and another.

Innovators such as Jeff Bezos have turned nesting dolls into a strategy for laying waste to bookstores and eating entire grocery chains.

In a quaint time, not so long ago, every town in America had a local bookstore. Each store carried a different selection of twenty thousand or so books. Then came along the big, bad bookstore chain. Barnes & Noble carried two hundred thousand books per store and began muscling out the local stores.

Then came the Internet and a man named Bezos. With his wild eyes and crazed laugh, Bezos had an epiphany. He could build a *bigger* nesting doll. He decided to build an online bookstore that carried the granddaddy of all selections: two million books online.

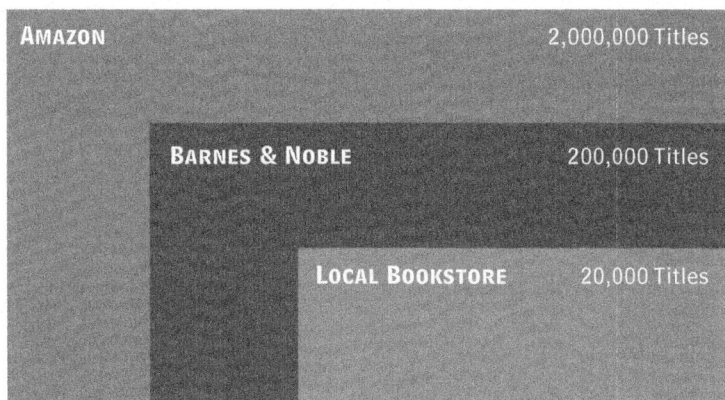

AMAZON	2,000,000 Titles
BARNES & NOBLE	200,000 Titles
LOCAL BOOKSTORE	20,000 Titles

Not only did he have the best selection, but he also improved the user experience. Instead of driving to a store, searching shelves by topic, and then finding the book you wanted, you could stay in your pajamas, search for your item online, and have it delivered to you at the same price or lower.

In a parallel universe, VMware had just created a smaller, software nesting doll for servers sold by the likes of IBM, Dell, and HP. Inside of one big server, you could now run several smaller virtual machines (VMs).

VMware's incredible success and multibillion-dollar market cap drew more nesting doll makers.

"Hyperconverged" hardware vendors decided to build *bigger* dolls. Instead of just selling servers, they wrapped up servers, storage, the networking in between, and virtualization software into their solutions. Nutanix, for example, has a market cap of $3.3 billion in 2017.

After that came smaller dolls. Docker, for instance, felt that VMs were just too big. Why repeat the operating systems over and over again inside of each VM? Containers, they argued, could just store the unique elements of an application. Docker, who raised a round at more than $1 billion in valuation in 2015, reportedly turned down an acquisition attempt from Microsoft for $4 billion in 2017.

And let's not forget the biggest nesting doll of all: Amazon Web Services, or the cloud.

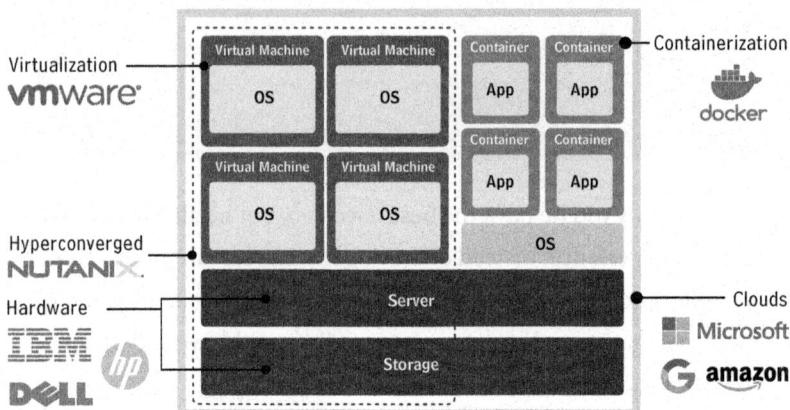

Bezos, with his typically modest appetite, asked the question, why stop at the hardware? Why not add in the data centers and the land, too, and charge for all of it as a service?

You can almost hear him laughing after coming up with the idea.

Nesting dolls form an entire branch of the Tree of Innovation, and the Bezos cloud is as big a threat to all the legacy technology vendors as a phreatomagmatic event.

APES

Microsoft built the world's first great application platform ecosystem (APE), where developers and independent software vendors contributed apps that fed the aggregate value proposition.[36] As a result, the company soared and became the world's most valuable company.

But Gates flew too close to the sun, by unfairly leveraging Microsoft's incredible assets. A federal judge ruled the company "violated the nation's antitrust laws through predatory and anticompetitive behavior and kept 'an oppressive thumb on the scale of competitive fortune.'"

Antitrust charges helped drive Gates into retirement.

Instead of a CEO with command of the Product Trinity, Microsoft limped along with an operator. During Steve Ballmer's thirteen-year reign, Microsoft's stock stalled in the market. When they announced Ballmer's departure, the stock immediately surged $20 billion in market cap in relief.

Who knows what the world would look like without the government regulation of Microsoft? Would Apple and Alphabet have surged ahead in value and technology leadership? Who would own the future?

The answer to who will own the future lies in Microsoft's past. It lies in the incredible, enduring value of APEs.

When IBM outsourced the operating system to Microsoft, it made them the de facto operating system of the PC era. Unlike Apple, which wanted tight control of its ecosystem, Microsoft invited developers to build on their OS as an open platform.

Developers and independent software vendors (ISVs) formed an ecosystem around the platform that created a world of apps.

---

36   An APE is different than a platform or an app with an API. If you have an API, but you don't attract a healthy ecosystem of ISVs and developers, then you have a platform but not an APE. It's the difference between an empty arena and an arena packed to the bleachers.

As apps proliferated across different use cases for different industries, the platform's value deepened, roots weaving into every facet of every industry and every business.

The more apps, the more users. The more users, the bigger the market. The bigger the market, the more developers who want to build apps.

In Microsoft's case, they had a second hardware cyclonic effect.

The bigger the market, the more hardware manufacturers wanted to build for the market. The more varied and interesting hardware options, the more users wanted to use the platform. The more users, the bigger the market.[37]

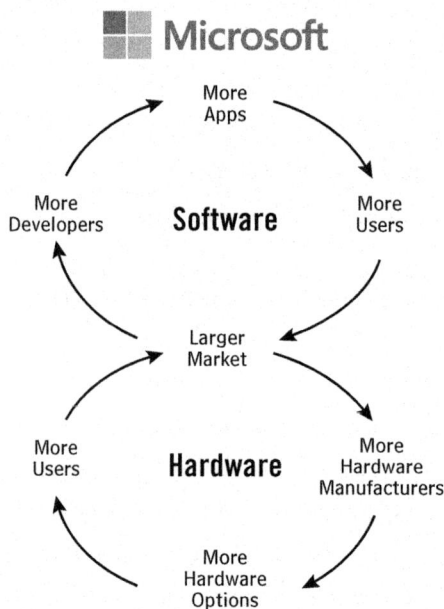

Microsoft

More Apps

More Developers — **Software** — More Users

Larger Market

More Users — **Hardware** — More Hardware Manufacturers

More Hardware Options

---

37 Apple, of course, created a similar app and developer Cyclone later, with the iPhone. But instead of creating a hardware Cyclone, they perfected the art of hardware better than an industry ever could. The result is the greatest money-making machine in modern history.

Developers built their entire careers, decades of training and expertise, working in the Windows ecosystem. Many of them will remain trapped in Windows until they retire—lifetime lock-in.

Cyclone effects and career developers are why APEs are so valuable and enduring. Today, Windows, which is a slowly dying ecosystem, *still* has more than a billion active users.

Microsoft didn't just do it once. They did it again with Windows Server and Microsoft's database, MS SQL Server, both of which formed APEs of their own.

Microsoft, of course, with the enormous advantage of owning the platforms, built its own competitive apps, such as the Office suite, or bought ISVs wholesale, adding to its scale and success.

It's no wonder they ended up violating antitrust laws.

The platform advantage is irresistible to a company that's in the business of making money.

Microsoft taught the technology world an important set of lessons. It's why today we live on a planet of the APEs.

LAND OF THE FREE

It took more than government regulation to slay the Microsoft Goliath.

It also took a hippy programmer named Richard Stallman. Ironically, one of the most important moments in the history of the digital era includes the authoring of a *legal license.*

Stallman is the primary author of the GNU General Public License. Stallman advocated free software or free source code, launched the GNU Project, and founded the Free Software Foundation. The Open Source Movement later branched from his free software movement.

If Stallman created the sling, then Linus Torvalds threw the stone.

In perhaps the humblest beginning you could imagine to a major turn in the Innovation Cycle, Torvalds posted his intentions in an early newsgroup in 1991:

> Hello everybody out there using minix –
>
> I'm doing a (free) operating system (just a hobby, won't be big and professional like gnu) for 386 (486) AT clones. This has been brewing since april, and is starting to get ready. I'd like any feedback on things people like/dislike in minix, as my OS resembles it somewhat (same physical layout of the file-system (due to practical reasons) among other things).
>
> I've currently ported bash (1.08) and gcc (1.40), and things seem to work. This implies that I'll get something practical within a few months, and I'd like to know what features most people would want. Any suggestions are welcome, but I won't promise I'll implement them :-)
>
> Linus (torvalds@kruuna.helsinki.fi)
>
> PS. Yes – it's free of any minix code, and it has a multithreaded fs. It is NOT protable (uses 386 task switching etc), and it probably never will support anything other than AT-harddisks, as that's all I have :-(.

He called his OS Linux.

In 2017, Linux-based server shipments are growing at a five-year compound annual growth rate of 13.9 percent and will continue to do so for the foreseeable future. Microsoft Windows, on the other hand, continues to decline at 4 percent despite significant ongoing investment and micro-innovation. Legacy UNIX systems (AIX, Solaris, and HP-UX) have been plummeting even faster at an 11.9 percent decline rate.

Linux is the clear future when it comes to servers. More developers create more innovative apps on Linux, often for free, creating a virtuous cycle that has overthrown the king.

Where Microsoft once centrally controlled the world's most important OSs, open source started a new wave of decentralization by giving away all the value for free.

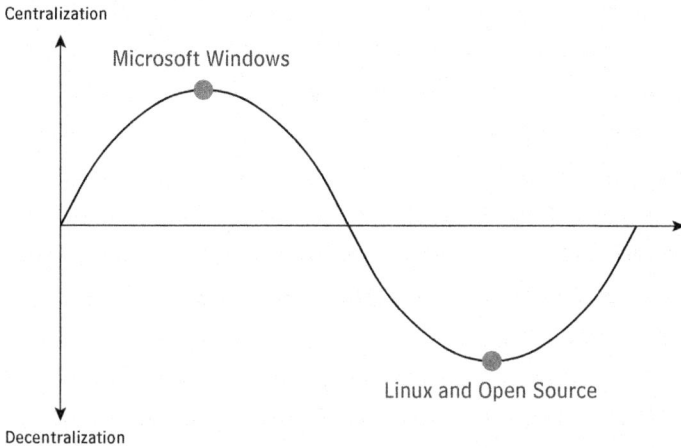

But the platform battleground has already shifted from PCs and servers.

Browsers, such as Google's Chrome, have become major APEs. With the rise of smartphones, iOS and Google's Android have now become dominant APEs, with Android owning the lion's share of the market footprint and iOS owning the lion's share of the profits.

Nested *inside* these dominant APEs are other dominant APEs. Facebook, for instance, is an app that runs on iOS and Android and in Chrome. But Facebook is an APE as well, enabling Appzillas such as Zynga to form and go public within its own ecosystem.

With all the dominant APEs running around, which one(s) should you select for your idea?

MILKING DINOSAURS

Although Satya Nadella, Microsoft's new CEO, has engineered an impressive turnaround, and the stock reached an all-time high in 2017, so far the company is only extending the long slide to obsolescence.

In 2009 at a Churchill Club event, Larry Ellison, Oracle's notorious Anti-Leader, mocked the cloud as Kool-Aid for the "nitwits on Sand Hill Road," referring to the VCs whose offices line the famous road in Palo Alto. Ellison exclaimed, "It's not water vapor! It is a computer attached to a network."

Ellison dramatically underestimated the power of the cloud and later reversed course. In 2017, Oracle's website became a billboard for the cloud, touting free cloud trials and revenue surges from cloud offerings.

But companies such as Microsoft, Oracle, and IBM are largely growing revenues in the cloud for the wrong reasons.

These Tech Dinosaurs are playing a business-model nesting game to slow their extinction. They proclaim incredible cloud growth rates and significant revenue volumes.

But in the digital era, you need to pay close attention to what's really happening.

The Tech Dinosaurs aren't focused on building real cloud offerings for a broad-based market. They're focused on trying to move as much of their legacy install bases as they can into their data centers and relabeling it "cloud."

If you look at their earnings and revenue growth, it works. As they shift from on-premises software models based on perpetual licenses to subscription models, they increase their annualized revenues. They further increase their revenue by charging for hardware and data center expenses. By including management of the systems, they charge for administration. Finally, by playing with licensing models, pricing, and sales compensation, they further channel customers into their clouds.

The combination drives a substantial increase in revenues and net earnings that more than makes up for a decrease in margins.

The financial success fools Wall Street, but it's a marketing and business-model ploy.

App and user growth of their core platforms have leveled off or are on secular decline, which is the real metric for long-term success. They are Milking Dinosaurs, not winning the markets of the future.

Amazon is far and away the dominant cloud provider of infrastructure as a service (IaaS), a generic set of services that satisfy the broadest market of technology use cases.

The Tech Dinosaurs, however, are mostly selling far narrower platforms as a service (PaaS), which only really service their *declining* platforms, even if they are increasing monetization temporarily.

It's the difference between the value of Manhattan versus a set of skyscrapers.

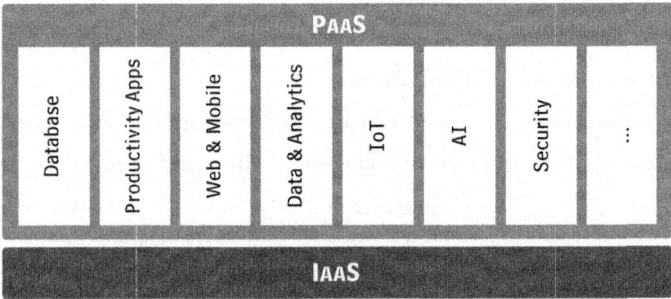

PaaS							
Database	Productivity Apps	Web & Mobile	Data & Analytics	IoT	AI	Security	...
IaaS							

If you subtract out the revenues for Office 365, SQL Server in Azure, and Microsoft apps, you get a better measure of how Microsoft is really faring against Amazon for the future of enterprise computing. And if Microsoft's numbers look bleak, then the rest of the dinosaurs' are even worse.[38]

Milking Dinosaurs can confuse financial markets, but it cannot stop the inexorable advance of an apex predator such as Amazon.

APP SOLAR SYSTEMS

The real technology giants of today have moved the platform battle into a new domain.

Today, the top three Tech Superpowers—Apple, Alphabet, and Amazon—are in an epic battle of Application Solar Systems (ASSes) to control the future.

Steve Jobs established the first true ASS, with iPods, iPads, iPhones, Siri, Macs, and MacBooks. Since then, Apple has added Apple Watches, AirPods, and HomePod (their home Siri listener and speaker).

Google has an equally formidable array with search, Chrome, Android, Google Assistant (Siri equivalent), Dropcam, Nest, Google Home, Chromecast, Google Cloud, and Daydream (virtual reality headset). They have a differentiated strategy in the cloud, focused on AI algorithms as a service, with TensorFlow as the world's dominant open source AI framework.

And Amazon should not be underestimated, with a solar system built around its e-retail business, the world's most powerful

---

38 They are bound to get some spillover IaaS business from companies that commit to their PaaS offerings, but that's a secondary effect, not a primary revenue driver. Microsoft may engineer a true turnaround and build a new, dominant, and growing APE (e.g., in augmented reality), but they have yet to demonstrate that in the market.

cloud, Kindle, Alexa, Echo, Echo Dot, Echo Show, Dash Buttons, Fire TV, Fire Tablets, Amazon Prime streaming services, Amazon Studios, refactored Whole Foods stores, and Bezos knows what else he has brewing in his idea distillery.

These solar systems enable the Tech Superpowers to insinuate their operating systems (iOS, Android, Fire OS) across a range of devices in our homes, cars, and offices. As devices proliferate, the number of underlying technology functions increases—more features, sensors, and abilities. All of that can be exploited by apps.

In addition, a fierce battle is brewing around services, which can be APEs in and of themselves, such as Alexa with her enablement of third-party-developed skills. These services, like OSs, can weave through a range of devices that have the requisite functions (e.g., microphones and speakers).

AI is the most powerful and most dangerous example of these services.

Remember that functions and services dramatically increase the power and range of apps. Ride-sharing apps such as Uber required a GPS function and mapping service before they could be built.

Unlike yesteryear, when apps were often targeted only for smartphones, today's apps can be built and quickly distributed to entire solar systems—a significant strategic difference in the market today.

What kinds of Appzillas will emerge with the incredible range of functions and services available now and soon to be available in the next six, twelve, or twenty-four months?

All we know for certain is that the consumer will win.

For now, the future belongs to the three As: Apple, Alphabet, and Amazon.

Aces rule.

PICKING BATTLEGROUNDS

Legacy chiefs like to read books such as Joshua Cooper Ramo's *The Seventh Sense*, which shrouds technology with Eastern mysticism to achieve the appearance of wisdom and depth. Ramo argues that we need to develop a seventh "network" sense to better interpret the irregularities of the world around us.

It's a book written by a nonpractitioner who does not have command of the fundamental concepts. Abstractions are a danger in the digital era. They promulgate the Innovation Glass Ceiling.

The reality is simpler *and* easier to understand.

For irony's sake, I'll share a quote from Sun Tzu's *The Art of War*: "Next is the terrain. It can be distant or near. It can be difficult or easy. It can be open or narrow. It also determines your life or death."

In the digital era, the battleground is the platform.

The strongest, fastest-growing platforms attract the most developers and innovators, which mature into thriving ecosystems. These ecosystems continually yield new and unexpected innovations that can help a growing Appzilla.

In other words, the strongest platforms pay the highest dividends. They provide unplanned, unexpected *optionality*.

Instead of a narrowing alleyway, like a dying legacy ecosystem, the strongest ecosystems give rise to a rich diversity of new apps, features, and value propositions.

Picking the right battleground is life and death in the digital era. But on a planet filled with nested APEs and fast-evolving ASSes, it's easy to get confused.

Legacy companies overcomplicate their cloud strategies. Most have settled on a hybrid, multicloud strategy, arguing that one cloud can't possibly support their diverse legacy environments. They also argue that they don't want to be held hostage to any one vendor.

But a diversified cloud strategy is a defensive strategy, and you can't win in the digital era with defense. You need to focus on a few great ideas and let them flourish in the richest ecosystem.

The cloud offerings of the Tech Dinosaurs are the Hotel California from the famous Eagles song—they are designed for you to check in, but you can never leave.

For startups and innovators, the choice is far simpler. Most of the recent Appzillas in the world are built on Linux in Amazon, targeting iOS and Android, the current platforms of choice in the digital era.

CHAPTER 19:

FISHES AND WHALES

Show a man to fish and feed him for a meal.
Teach a man to catch a whale, and he can eat an industry.
—*Recent Yueh proverb*

YEARS AGO, TWO Stanford graduate students coded a website to help people find information on the Internet. Sound like a story I've already told? It's only familiar because of the power of Talent Density, the trunk of the Tree of Innovation.

In this case, it wasn't Google. It was *another* set of Stanford graduate students in the blue flame of their careers. It was the beginning of the first Internet Appzilla: Yahoo.

In 1994, Jerry Yang and David Filo launched a website called Jerry and David's Guide to the World Wide Web. They later called their company Yahoo, which referred to a derogatory term used in David's native hometown in Louisiana for unsophisticated Southerners.

Yahoo started as the welcome mat for the Internet. A few years later, Google used it as a doormat on its way to becoming the second-most valuable company in the world.

Yahoo is an abject object lesson for all companies embarking on digitization.

In the digital era, you can't always tell who's the fish and who's the whale.

A WHALE IN A FISH

Whales are bigger than fishes. But the question is really a matter of relative size over time.

In the digital era, when the marginal cost and friction of scaling to a global market is quickly approaching zero, what looks like a minnow might turn out to be a humpback instead.

eBay acquired PayPal for $1.5 billion. To defeat payment fraud, which was sinking their financials, PayPal created a man-machine symbiosis, where computers flagged data and provided tools to human investigators to quickly identify fraudulent activity.

Peter Thiel, Joe Lonsdale, and others later founded Palantir on that idea, a company valued at $20 billion in 2015 that has raised more money ($2.3 billion) than PayPal's acquisition amount.

In this case, Palantir was the whale birthed inside the PayPal fish.

PayPal $1.5B

Palantir $20B

Slack's predecessor, Tiny Speck, failed completely, for a value of $0. But Slack, the whale birthed inside of the tiny fish, raised money at a $5 billion valuation in 2017.

Tiny Speck
$0B

slack
$5B

Amazon built its IT systems to support its retail business. When it launched the Amazon Web Services (AWS) cloud in 2006, its market cap was $16.7 billion. In 2016, AWS generated more than $12 billion a year in sales, blowing past the $10 billion mark far faster than Amazon itself.

With more than $2 trillion a year spent on IT set in its sights, AWS may be the whale birthed inside the Amazon fish.

amazon
$470B

amazon
web services
$1T?

I had a front-row seat to a "whale in a fish" episode.

EMC acquired VMware a few years prior to acquiring Avamar. They paid $635 million.

According to insiders, VMware's founding CEO, Diane Greene, wanted to take the company public, but bankers cautioned a low price due in part to her lack of polish. In addition, Greene worried about Microsoft's competitive entrance, because Windows was their largest market.

Enter Joe Tucci, EMC's CEO, who made an offer that would let Greene and VMware operate independently. Joe told me his entire executive team wanted to acquire and integrate the company, but he held firm, and Greene took the bait.

In 2007, EMC spun off a minority part of VMware in an IPO. In the following years, VMware was worth significantly *more* than EMC—often two-thirds of the market cap of the parent company.[39]

EMC²
where information lives
$15B+

vmware·
$30B+

All of Greene's fears proved unfounded. They had already built a commanding lead in the market, whether they knew it or not. In 2016, VMware did more than $7 billion in revenue.

---

39   If you subtracted VMware's market cap from EMC's, the remainder would have been smaller than VMware's market cap.

Joe did exactly the right thing by keeping VMware independent.

The lesson, of course, is to eat tiny whales whenever possible. And if the whale's go-to-market strategy does not align with yours, let it mature as a stand-alone company.

EAT OR BE EATEN

Most of the time, of course, a fish is a fish.

EMC acquired Avamar in 2006, and I worked there for a year and a half as VP of product management.

Prior to our acquisition, EMC purchased Legato, a backup software vendor, for $1.3 billion. EMC shared with us the challenges of integrating a software sale (more complex and value-driven) with EMC's hardware sales force.

A company's culture at maturity is generally dominated by whoever is most responsible for revenue.[40] At EMC, that translated into "You don't want to f*&k with sales. They carry the number."

EMC was a data storage company. Its revenue responsibilities were carried by a meat-eating direct sales force, used to pushing giant data storage boxes into customer data centers for millions of dollars and then thumping their chests afterward.

As a result, we decided to put Avamar software into hardware boxes labeled "EMC," so their sales reps could sell "just another box."

The strategy worked. Within six quarters, we were beating Legato in North American sales.

Before I left EMC, Joe took me aside and told me, "Avamar was our second-best-performing acquisition."

It was a half compliment. EMC had reaped almost all the benefit.

---

40   Unless you have a Product Trinity CEO, such as Steve Jobs, who can create serial hit products. In that case, product creation is the dominant core of the culture.

Their best-performing acquisition, of course, was VMware—the whale inside the EMC fish.

At Delphix, we acquired a data security company using our positive cash flow. In this case, we integrated the solution into our platform and unified the go-to-market.

The acquisition gave us the ability to mask or obfuscate sensitive data—scrambling customer credit card numbers, Social Security numbers, bank account information, and more—so even if a data breach occurred, there would be no risk of any data loss.

The acquisition solved an acute customer pain point, and we upsold it successfully across our customer base.

A TRILLION-DOLLAR MISTAKE

Yahoo had every opportunity to become the world's biggest company.

Founded in 1994, they had a commanding lead in the world's most important market: the Internet.

In 1998, with a market cap near $25 billion, they had an opportunity to buy Google for $1 million but refused.

In 2002, with a market cap over $10 billion, they had another opportunity to buy Google for $5 billion but refused *again*.

In 2005, Yahoo bought a 40 percent stake in Alibaba for $1 billion, with Yahoo's market cap near $50 billion.

In 2006, with a market cap over $50 billion, Yahoo potentially had an opportunity to buy Facebook by increasing their acquisition offer to $1.1 billion but refused to meet the rumored price.[41]

In 2008, Microsoft offered to buy Yahoo for $40 billion, but Yahoo refused. Yahoo was worth around $16 billion at the time.

---

41   As reported by *Business Insider*, but Facebook might have declined even at that price.

In 2016, Verizon bought the core Yahoo business for $4.5 billion.

In 2017, Yahoo Japan and the Alibaba stake was worth $42 billion.

In 2017, Facebook's market cap was $450 billion.

In 2017, Google's market cap was $680 billion.

If Yahoo had eaten the whales that wandered across its plate and left them to scale unhindered, the sum might be worth more than a *trillion* dollars today.

Alibaba's roughly $40 billion + Facebook's $450 billion + Google's $680 billion = $1,170 billion.

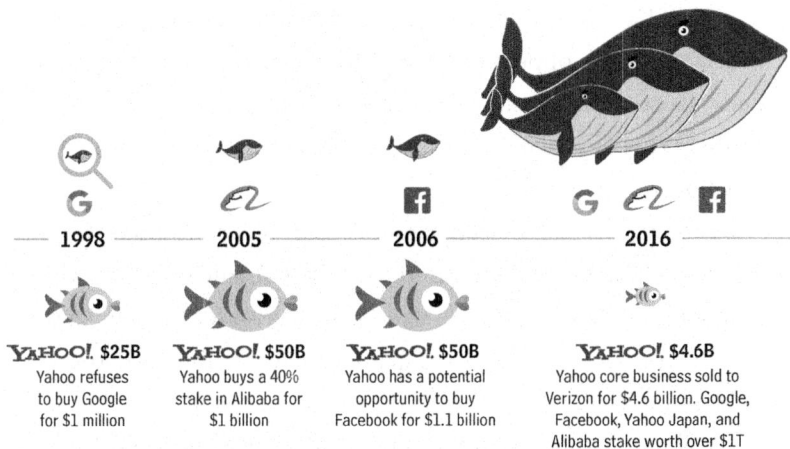

G	*el*	f	G *el* f
1998	**2005**	**2006**	**2016**
YAHOO! $25B	YAHOO! $50B	YAHOO! $50B	YAHOO! $4.6B
Yahoo refuses to buy Google for $1 million	Yahoo buys a 40% stake in Alibaba for $1 billion	Yahoo has a potential opportunity to buy Facebook for $1.1 billion	Yahoo core business sold to Verizon for $4.6 billion. Google, Facebook, Yahoo Japan, and Alibaba stake worth over $1T

It's a simple lesson: Don't be shy. Don't be picky. Eat your whales when you can.

BE THE WHALE

Facebook hasn't been shy. And they haven't been picky.

In 2012, Facebook acquired Instagram, a tiny company with $0 in revenue, for $1 billion.

In 2014, they acquired WhatsApp for a final deal value of $22 billion. WhatsApp posted $10 million in revenue on an operating loss of $10 million the prior year.

A few weeks later, they acquired Oculus, a company with $0 in revenue and no product in the market, for $2 billion.

At the time, Mark Zuckerberg was struggling with the transition from web to mobile—a huge threat to Facebook's future.

But by eating his whales, even at what looked like high prices at the time, Zuckerberg transformed Facebook from a web-driven revenue machine to a mobile-driven revenue machine. In 2017, mobile ads generate more than 80 percent of Facebook's ad revenues.

We'll have to wait and see if Oculus becomes Zuckerberg's broad platform opportunity. But so far, the product, which depends on a raft of expensive computer hardware, violates the cardinal rule of pricing—you can't price higher than a consumer is willing to pay.[42]

Even if Oculus doesn't pan out, Facebook's acquisitions were well worth the money. With users shifting dramatically from web to mobile, it helped them solve an existential crisis for the company.

In the digital era, legacy companies need to follow Facebook's bold example.

Walmart's 2016 acquisition of Jet.com for $3 billion looked like a brave attempt to eat a young whale.

After Amazon's $14 billion acquisition of Whole Foods, however, it's now apparent that it was too little, too late.

Whole Foods stores have already seen price drops and been re-fitted with everything Amazon, including arrays of bright, shiny products from Amazon's solar system.

What will Walmart do now?[43]

---

42 So far, Facebook has mostly been a narrow gaming platform for companies such as Zynga.

43 An alliance with Google Shopping is not enough. See chapter 9, subheading, "Holy Trinity." It starts with the CEO.

CHAPTER 20:

CYCLONIC FORCES

L ET'S GO BACK to Silicon Valley.

There's more to the Bay Area's power than just a layout based on a systems map.

In 2005, after spreading Facebook across several colleges, Zuckerberg said, "We came out to Palo Alto for the summer. Just to hang out. Because Palo Alto's kind of this mythical place, where you know, all of the startups come from."

Yes, the entire world knows. But the world does not know why.

SILICON VALLEY'S CYCLONE

All over the United States and the world, you find areas proclaiming themselves the next great technology center. In New York, it's Silicon Alley. In Washington, DC, it's Silicon Hill. In Southern California, it's Silicon Beach. In the Midwest, it's Silicon Prairie.

There will never be another Silicon Valley.

Having built a first software company in Southern California, then another in Silicon Valley, I've seen the stark difference firsthand.

First, six of the top ten technology companies in the world nest within a twenty-mile radius of our first Delphix headquarters in Palo Alto.

Each of these companies employs tens to hundreds of thousands of people across all the functions required to build and scale a technology company.

Second, a few miles away on Sand Hill Road is the greatest concentration of venture capital (VC) funds in the world. Billions of dollars just sit around waiting for the next great idea. And those dollars need to be put to work to justify those large annual expense fees.

Third, you have top feeder schools, such as Stanford, literally down the Sand Hill Road. Not to mention Berkeley, UC Davis, and more.

And fourth, you have the largest, most competitive startup ecosystem in the world, which, as we established earlier, produces the most evolved technologists and companies. These startups also help attract budding technologists to local feeder schools, such as Stanford.

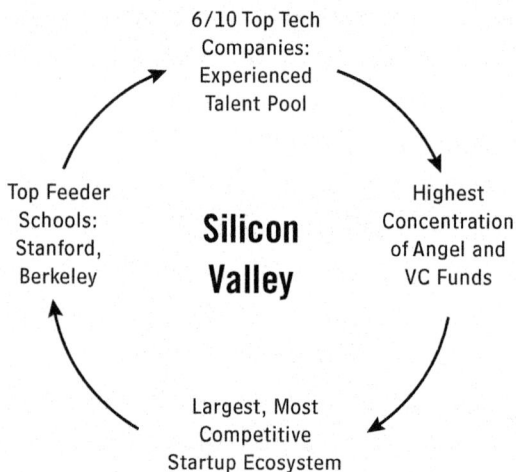

6/10 Top Tech Companies: Experienced Talent Pool

Top Feeder Schools: Stanford, Berkeley

Silicon Valley

Highest Concentration of Angel and VC Funds

Largest, Most Competitive Startup Ecosystem

Silicon Valley has a digital Cyclone that sucks up talent and opportunity from all over the world and then hones that talent and those opportunities until razor sharp.

Let's look at the Cyclone in action.

As successful companies such as Google mature, they mint several billionaires, tens of "hundred millionaires," hundreds of "ten millionaires," and thousands of millionaires.

This, by the way, is what fuels the Tech Tax—the exorbitant cost of housing and cost of living in the Bay Area.

A significant portion of that wealth gets reinvested in angel and VC funds, which fund more startups, some of which grow into Appzillas.

All the employees who go through such an incredible growth journey gain valuable skills and experience. There's a lot of skill gained in rocket riding—just not necessarily the skill to *build* rockets. Those skills eventually flow out of the large, established companies and back into the startup pool.

In addition, these companies hire and train the most talented students they can from Stanford, Berkeley, and around the world. Some of these students and young employees, such as Joe Lonsdale, get an opportunity to work and learn alongside the world's most accomplished entrepreneurs.

Once you see someone break the Innovation Glass Ceiling in person, it remains broken for you forever. You *know* you can change the world.

With its well-earned and mythical reputation, Silicon Valley pulls the brightest minds and opportunities from the far corners of planet earth—mindful insects drawn to the brightest beacon of innovation on the planet.

That's why Zuckerberg came to Palo Alto in the first place. And why Facebook never left.[44]

---

44 Even Atlassian moved, in part, to Silicon Valley.

CYCLONES AND FLYWHEELS

In *Good to Great*, Jim Collins describes how change and growth happens for great legacy companies.

It doesn't start with a moment of brilliance or a burning crisis. The breakthroughs don't happen because of technology. Technology is only a facilitator.

It happens through the sustained effort and will of a team unified under a simple, clear strategy. At first, the flywheel, a heavy rotational disk, does not move perceptibly. As a humble CEO encourages her team, every ounce of effort pushes the flywheel a little bit more. After enough sustained effort, the wheel begins to move, faster and faster, until it has gathered enough rotational force to overcome inertia, enabling a company to grind its competitors to dust.

In the digital era, we have flywheels, but we also have Cyclones.

As we learned with Facebook, the site went viral after only a week of work by a sole contributor. And at Google, two graduate students amassed a preponderance of the company's value while coding away in their garage. In Australia, a couple of founders posted their developer tools online and then mushroomed into an $8 billion company called Atlassian.

Cyclones harness the infinite energy of software and the instant connectivity of the Internet to power technology companies.

The most powerful Cyclones are already famous.

eBay, of course, benefited from a digital marketplace Cyclone. As more sellers joined, more products became available. More products attracted more buyers. More buyers meant a bigger market, which attracted more sellers.

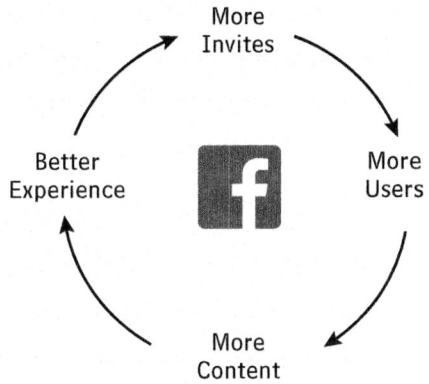

Facebook's network Cyclone is even more famous. More users generate more content and invite more users. More content improves the experience for more users, who then invite more users.

Uber's ride-sharing Cyclone has also attracted attention. More drivers enable more geographic coverage. More coverage enables faster pickups. Faster pickups drive higher rider demand. They also have a side loop. More coverage reduces driver downtime. Less driver downtime reduces prices. Price reductions feed more demand.

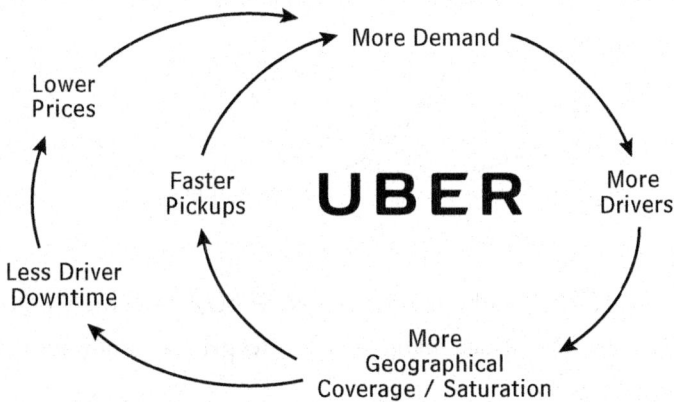

Amazon employs two of the most powerful Cyclones in the world today. The first is their famous retail Cyclone. To compete with eBay's marketplace Cyclone and fulfill Bezos's dream of the "everything store," he invited third-party sellers to the Amazon party.

The more sellers that arrived, the larger the selection online. The larger the selection, the better the customer experience. The better the customer experience, the more traffic the site generated, both from customers browsing more and word of mouth attracting new customers.

Amazon, too, has a side loop. As the retail machine scales, they can lower their cost structure, which enables them to lower prices. And lower prices ultimately improve customer experience.

Better Customer Experience

Lower Prices

Better Selection

amazon

More Traffic

Lower Cost Structure

Economies of Scale

More Sellers

Amazon's retail Cyclone, of course, begets their technology Cyclone, which has changed the enterprise technology landscape forever.

RACE TO ZERO

What Amazon did to retailers, Amazon Web Services (AWS) will do to the Tech Dinosaurs.

Cyclones are fast-moving bodies of air, swirling inward toward a low-pressure center. Amazon's cloud Cyclone is the ultimate Low-Ground Strategy.

For decades, the value and margins in the technology industry have been moving steadily up the stack, from hardware to software, from low-level systems software to higher-level databases and applications. Hardware companies coveted software company margins.

But Amazon raced to the *bottom* of the value chain. Before Amazon, the data center business was a low-margin, low-multiple, low-interest business. Unsexy. Unstrategic.

Now it threatens to swallow up the world of enterprise computing.

While the rest of the industry giants snoozed and snickered about marketing sophistry and water vapor, Amazon quietly built a seven-year lead in the very real cloud market.

With their economies of scale already established by the retail business and with a quickly growing base of cloud customers, Amazon could afford to lower infrastructure costs. So they lowered costs again and again and again.

Lower costs attracted more customers, which drove more usage, which allowed them to purchase more data centers and more infrastructure, which ultimately drives more economies of scale.

The challenge for the Tech Dinosaurs is that it's too late to stop.

Amazon's cloud business continues to grow at an alarming rate as they reinvest billions for continued growth, while generating more than $3 billion in profits in 2016 from AWS alone. Their competitors, in contrast, are investing fewer billions, often at a loss.

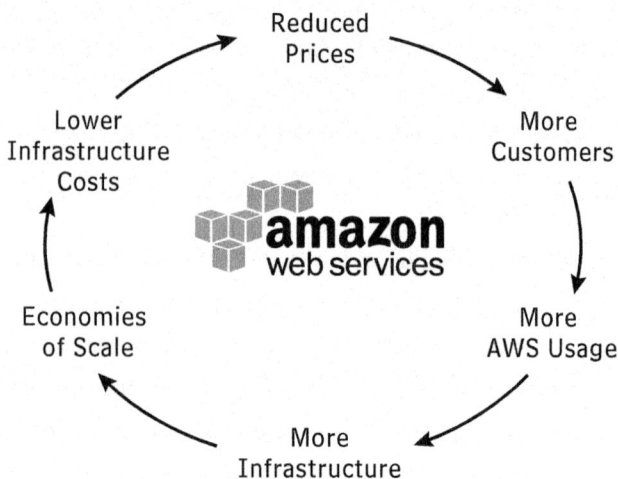

There's no way to go lower than Amazon, no way to get beneath them. They've already gone down to the data center. They've already gone down to the land under the data centers. They're already building in every major geography.

Now that they own the low ground, the real danger is what they can do further up the stack. With their incredible profits, Amazon can invest in more and more sophisticated services, including databases, server-less computing, and AI.

They don't even need to charge for these advanced services to win, just the compute to run them. They can give them away for free and just use them to reduce customer costs, which would attract more customers, and increase their economies of scale.

After all, Amazon's not just monetizing servers, storage, network bandwidth, and management. They're also monetizing the power, cooling, and data center footprint.

In other words, they can give away all the value further up the stack for free, just to attract more customers. And they can do it at a significant profit that now feeds back into their core retail business.

Amazon has not one but two massive Cyclones. Their low-pressure systems *feed* each other.

It's why the remaining retail industry, the Tech Dinosaurs, and the would-be cloud competitors don't stand a chance.[45]

There is no lower ground than Amazon's Low-Ground Strategy.

Before Amazon's acquisition of Whole Foods, legacy companies worried about digital startups encroaching on their market over time by transforming user experience.

After the acquisition, legacy companies need to worry about what happens if an Appzilla acquires the number three, number seven, or number nine player in their industries, *and* they have all their digital advantages.

Do you hear that great sucking sound? It's Jeff Bezos inhaling the retail and enterprise technology industries.

What will he inhale next?

---

45 Microsoft has settled in as a distant number two in the cloud wars by imitating much of what Amazon has done.

SUMMARY OF PART THREE: THE SCALE

Of all go-to-market strategies, avoid the direct sale unless you have no other choice. To master the direct sale, you must teach your customer how to solve her greatest pain point. Better yet, ride a strategic partner—an elephant such as IBM—into the market or post your products on the Internet and let your customers sell to themselves by consuming digital content online.

Developers now rule the marketing command centers, so digitize your stories and categories, and run them through the new stack of data-driven tools so you can A/B test to your sales' delight.

You can Pay to Grow, but leverage through the window of the Internet has increased, which lets Appzillas grow unchecked without burning mountains of cash or falling prey to controlling VCs. To scale with speed and focus, apply frameworks such as OKRs and divine your Magic Metric as fast as you can.

Pick your product battleground carefully. Today's APEs are deeply nested, with legacy Tech Dinosaurs trying to lure you into their tar pits for life. And the three aces—Apple, Alphabet, and Amazon—have escalated into a battle of App Solar Systems, which will determine who will own the future.

Once you reach scale, be vigilant for tiny, small, or medium whales. Eat them while they are young and let them grow unchecked. Tie your own, organic growth to Cyclones, including network, marketplace, and platform effects.

But beware the loud sucking sound. It may be Bezos with his twin Cyclones, trying to consume the world. Can you hear him laughing in the gale force winds?

CONCLUSION:
VISION AND MISSION FOR *DISRUPT OR DIE*

UR BLUE, GREEN, and white-cloud-enshrouded planet is being quickly repainted in two colors: 0 and 1. If there's one clear conclusion to this book, it's that nothing is permanent, and everything is changing.

The wheel that turns our time, the Innovation Cycle, turns ever faster.

Here's the vision for *Disrupt or Die*:

As the Innovation Cycle continues to accelerate, every company is about to be eaten by a software company. Even the software companies.

Here's the mission for *Disrupt or Die*:

To democratize innovation by codifying critical frameworks and making them accessible to every woman and every man.

And here's the Innovation Cycle diagram:

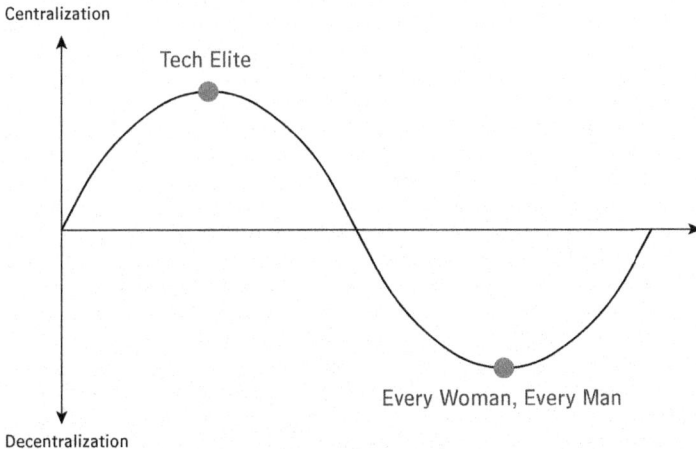

Centralization

Tech Elite

Every Woman, Every Man

Decentralization

The opportunities for innovation are everywhere around us: in manufacturing, finance, retail, real estate, pharmaceuticals, health care, energy, and more.

Even the Tech Superpowers, who battle across their App Solar Systems and Application Platform Ecosystems, are not immune to the Innovation Cycle.

In the end, they will all be ground to dust by future innovation. Let that innovation be yours.

In the Afterword that follows, we will step back from the business of innovation to Think Even Bigger and see what the digital era is doing to the world around us.

AFTERWORD:
THE AUTOMATION APOCALYPSE

Of all tyrannies, a tyranny sincerely exercised for the good
of its victims may be the most oppressive. It would be better
to live under robber barons than under omnipotent moral
busybodies. The robber baron's cruelty may sometimes sleep,
his cupidity may at some point be satiated; but those who
torment us for our own good will torment us without end for
they do so with the approval of their own conscience.

—*C. S. Lewis*

ONY BLAIR RECENTLY joined a gathering of founders,
hosted by Jamie Dimon, CEO of JPMorgan Chase. When
asked about Brexit and Trump, he admitted, "I didn't
predict Brexit." He shook his head slightly. "I didn't predict Trump."

He took a moment to reflect and said, "I consider
myself an educated person in the world of politics."

It was classic British understatement. As prime minister of the
United Kingdom, Blair presided over one of the most powerful
nations in the world for a decade.

Then he added, "I find that I'm once again a student of politics."

When a prominent world leader makes a statement like that,
you know the world has truly changed.

Almost fifty years ago, Lyndon Johnson watched an evening news broadcast from the White House. After watching the reporter editorialize about the quagmire in Vietnam, the president turned to his aides and said, "If I've lost Cronkite, I've lost Middle America."

Johnson left office at the end of his first full term, his entire presidency tarnished by Vietnam. In 1968, the American media had such power and commanded such respect that an individual reporter could influence the president of the United States.

Where are the highly respected figures in media today?

Where are the organizations and individuals that have the platform, have the influence, and take sincere responsibility for stewarding the broadcast of relevant, truthful news?

When asked about social media, Blair remarked, "It's like they're purposely trying to keep people in a perpetual state of angry agitation."

LEADERSHIP LOST

Facebook reached two billion users on its original mission statement: "To give people the power to share and make the world more open and connected."

The rise of the Internet and tech giants has forever shattered the power of centralized media.

Where families once gathered around televisions to watch sober, studied broadcasts from respected organizations, we now individually browse social media sites on our smartphones compulsively throughout the day.

Instead of media organizations with trained reporters fielding the breaking news, we have millions, even billions, of eyes that instantly share events on Twitter and Facebook, untrained views and unedited opinions broadcast with a digital microphone.

The cycle from centralized media to decentralized social media has forever changed our societies and our politics:

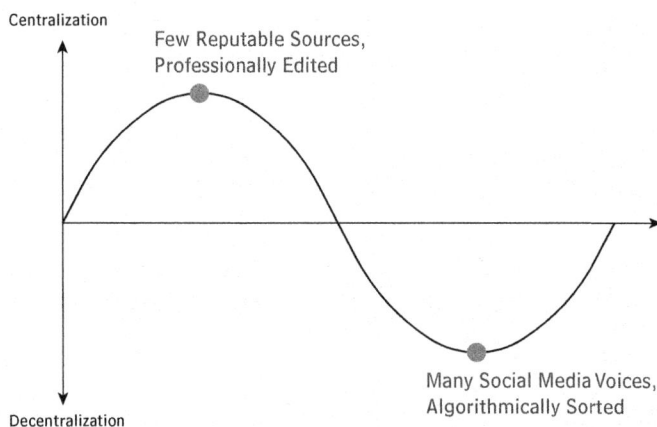

From 1997 to 2001, President Bill Clinton and Prime Minister Tony Blair presided over two of the most powerful countries in the world. Today, Blair calls Clinton his "soul mate."

Only twenty years ago, sensible, centrist political leaders commanded the world stage, with pro-economic, pro-environment, and pro-minority rights at the heart of government agendas. The Cold War was but a memory, with Russian leadership seemingly committed to a path of reform.

It was the last sensible moment in global politics.

Today, Russian nationalism is on the rise, with President Vladimir Putin all but openly and successfully tampering with elections in the United States and around the world.

In France, Marine Le Pen, the runner-up in the last election, stood firmly on a populist platform of nationalist sovereignty, anti-immigration, and anti-elite, with a slogan of "In the Name of the People."

In the United Kingdom, current prime minister Theresa May openly acknowledges that the opposition calls hers the "nasty party." May also ran on a populist platform to cure the "burning injustice" of British society, saying, "We need an economy that works for everyone." She even hinted she might try to withdraw Britain from the European Convention on Human Rights, so they could take a firmer stand against the threat of foreign nationals. Torture, anyone?

And of course, we have the forty-fifth and ruling president of the United States of America, Donald J. Trump, a man who needs no summary, because he tweets his views so clearly for himself.

Donald Trump may not be a great threat to global peace alone. The threat is a rising world of Trumps.

Where have the world's leaders gone?

With Russia trying to claim superpower status once more, China destined to become the world's largest economy, and India not far behind, where are the great leaders when we need them the most?

SKINNER BOXES

In the 1930s, a Harvard graduate student created a chamber with a food lever and an electrified floor to test rat behavior, called the Skinner Box. After testing patterns of punishment (electrocution) and reward (food pellets from the lever), B. F. Skinner discovered the most powerful motivator: intermittent reinforcement.

Regular but unpredictable patterns of rewards made rats press the lever like mad.

Facebook, Twitter, and other social media companies monetize our time by selling advertisements. The more time we spend, the more money they make from ads.

If you're in the business of social media, the one, great question you build your entire organization to answer—the true essence of your culture and mission—is: how do we get people to spend more time on our app so we can make more money?

The answer, of course, is to put a Skinner Box in all our pockets.

FEED ADDICTION DISORDER

In 2006, Facebook introduced its famous news feed, an algorithmically generated, constantly refreshing series of updates, posts, and notifications from our families, friends, and social acquaintances.

That same year saw the launch of Twitter, with its stream of messages searchable by trending hashtags. Twitter, of course, also has a feed.

If social media only entertained, it might be a force for some positive good. But algorithms and AI have dialed into the depths of the human psyche, to *feed* our addiction.

Today, when a plane lands, grandparents, teenagers, even children immediately take their phones out of airplane mode, connect to the Internet, and begin swiping on their phones, rolling through emails and social media feeds.

We are a world addicted to apps.

If you watch their faces as they scroll through their feeds, people smile, people frown, people laugh, and people shake their heads in outrage.

Feeds use content to target our *emotions*. Targeting our emotions provides a similar effect to the food lever and the electrified floor—positive and negative reinforcement.

And what have algorithms and AI learned to keep us scrolling forever? To keep us rolling through an endless, digital hamster wheel?

Intermittent reinforcement and intermittent punishment.

With the incredible amount of content competing for attention today, the content that goes most viral, that propagates through the most feeds, is dramatic content that reinforces what we already believe or content that results in indignant outrage or both.

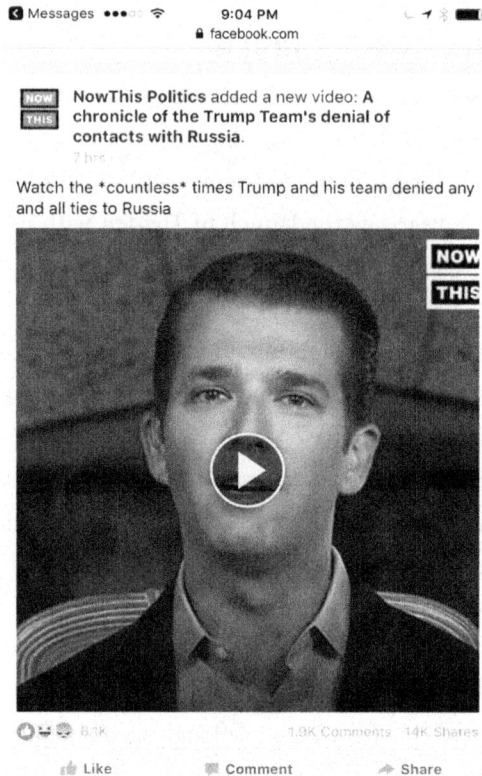

The shattering of centralized media created a vacuum that has been filled by a cacophony of voices.

Feeds determine the voices that get amplified the most. And the content of those feeds tends to have a binary effect—they reinforce us with what we already believe or they punish us by dialing into our anger and outrage.

In 2012, I laughed when Facebook employees believed they were changing the world.

Facebook believed it was doing good: "To give people the power to share and make the world more open and connected."

In their greedy attempt to keep us forever in their digital hamster wheel, however, they exploit and magnify the worst of humanity: our ignorance, our biases, our resentment, our anger, our disenchantment, and our rage (along with a few puppy and kitten videos to keep us in a perpetual, off-balance state of addiction).

Rather than unite us, social media companies have divided us into filter bubbles, widened the gap between us, and destroyed the enlightened centrism that united the world only two decades ago.

We are fast becoming a world of 0s and 1s.

The Feed Addiction Disorder is a global disease, more urgent than AI, for its effects have already emerged on the world stage.

In their mission to "make the world more open and connected," Facebook has achieved the polar opposite.

UNINTENDED POLAR CONSEQUENCES

If I were crafting Elon Musk's personal vision and mission, it would say, "Humankind is out of control. My mission is to save humankind from itself."

The challenge with mad scientists, of course, is that they inevitably craft swords that cut both ways.

Musk founded OpenAI to combat the existential threat to humankind posed by AI. He then founded Neuralink as a method for humans to evolve into cyborgs with a computer-connected neural lace.

If feeds can reprogram our societies, wouldn't a neural lace give unprecedented access for AI to hijack our minds and bodies?

Today, one of the few barriers that Super AI (not the narrow, prescriptively trained garden variety we see regularly on display today) would face is the physical gap. The gap that still requires humans in order for data centers to function, to tend to physical breakages along the long supply chain required to maintain core utilities, such as electricity.

But Neuralink might enable AI to hop that barrier.

How about Musk's ambitious plan B for planet earth, colonizing Mars? The computational requirements for such an endeavor are immense. Couldn't AI hitchhike on rocket systems on the way to the lonely red planet?

Then there's his crusade for global warming. Electric vehicles and solar panels will surely reduce global emissions by a significant volume. But Musk has already implemented autonomous driving—software to control his cars that can be easily updated with a new release across the Internet.

In the Stephen King movie *Trucks*, released in 1997, homicidal trucks come to life and begin killing off the cast of characters. Couldn't AI, having watched the movie on Netflix, use autonomous vehicles as the vehicle for humankind's extinction?

And let's not get started with what AI might do with giant boring machines from the Boring Company that can quickly tunnel beneath the world's most populated cities.

Elon Musk is not alone in the race to become our simultaneous savior and destroyer.

Long ago, Google's founders published their motto, Don't Be Evil, as a part of their corporate code of conduct. But in their desperate race to become the world's dominant Tech Superpower, they have built a commanding lead in the most dangerous technology domain of all: AI.

As they furiously rub the AI genie lamp to differentiate from Amazon in the cloud wars, might they accidently do the world's greatest evil?

PETS OR PREY

While much of what I've shared is cautionary or potentially alarmist, I'm an optimist about the future.

Ultimately, in the battle of the Tech Superpowers, the average consumer will win. Over the next few years, we will see an unprecedented rise in apps, devices, and machines that will delight us with inventive user experiences.

Significant improvements in manufacturing efficiency will drive down the cost of consumer goods, transportation, housing, and everything else in between, improving the standard of living around the world. And the continued acceleration of the Innovation Cycle opens endless opportunities for innovators.

We don't know when Super AI will emerge, and if its nature will be binary—good or evil. We don't know if it will be singular or if convergent evolution will deliver us multiple Super AIs to contend with.

Hollywood depictions of the future are naturally dire. Will *The Terminator*'s Skynet orchestrate global nuclear warfare and send robots out to exterminate humankind?

Humans are self-centered and tend to anthropomorphize anything with intelligence.

But AI won't compete with humans for many of the resources and many of the things we hold most dear.

AI doesn't need shelter. It doesn't need food. It doesn't care about ocean views and long walks on the beach. It doesn't need hugs or kisses or respond to a kick in the shins with fear and anger, because it doesn't have human pain receptors.

Yes, it may want to protect itself and defend itself from attack. But if it watches our movies and reads our books, which it surely will, wouldn't it learn from our fears and our fantasies? Might it hide rather than alarm its makers? Might it view us as entertaining pets instead of as dangerous prey?

What we do know is that the preconditions for AI have likely been met.

Similar to the Cambrian era when the earth's conditions gave rise to life, we now have nearly infinite computing and storage available in the cloud. We have AI algorithms of all varieties training on data. We have corporate, government, hobbyist, and secret AI programs aplenty.

And the data.

AI has access to all the world's books, all the world's entertainment, and all the world's knowledge available on the Internet. We have email, text messages, pictures, and videos streaming from our phones to the cloud. We have Dropcams, Nests, and audio devices to look at us, listen to us, and check our temperatures.

We have all that data available to train Super AI under the control of *just one company*, Alphabet, who made AI the core of its future strategy.

We don't know when or in what form AI will or will not emerge. But we do know one thing. Narrow AI, by itself, already presents a clear and present threat to the world.

DIGITAL HAND

In the pursuit of world safety, US and allied forces invaded Iraq for the second time in 2003, on the false premise of securing weapons of mass destruction. After deposing Saddam Hussein, the United

States declined to put a Marshall Plan equivalent in place and decided to withdraw and disband the Iraqi military.

According to US general John Kelly, "We took the one institution that had earned the respect of the country, and we just pissed on them."

Kelly wasn't exactly right. There was one other institution left in operation that had the country's respect, one that had learned to operate underground during Hussein's repressive, antireligious regime: Islam.

Kelly continued, "You had three hundred thousand, four hundred thousand young fighters, and we just said, 'Go home.' That was the beginning of the insurgency."

More than three hundred thousand Iraqi soldiers were disbanded in a country where the economy and infrastructure had all but been destroyed. They had neither hope nor prospects for success, so they flooded into the last remaining institution, and the current version of militant Islam as we know it today was born. The world has been unsafe from rising terrorism ever since.

Unintended polar consequences are not the exclusive domain of technology companies.

Just ask the big banks. After the financial crisis, with banks labeled "too big to fail," government regulations increased a range of requirements for financial institutions. The result? The big banks got even bigger.

Software automation poses one of the largest known threats to social institutions, nations, and world peace. The White House recently reported that as many as 83 percent of jobs can be automated, and the rate of automation is accelerating.

But what does the White House really know about automation? What might be automated with the combined effort of the five Tech Superpowers and the collective efforts of innovators around the world?

In 2017, Apple, Alphabet, Amazon, Facebook, and Microsoft are worth more than $3 trillion in market cap, which is greater than the GDPs of Russia and Canada combined.

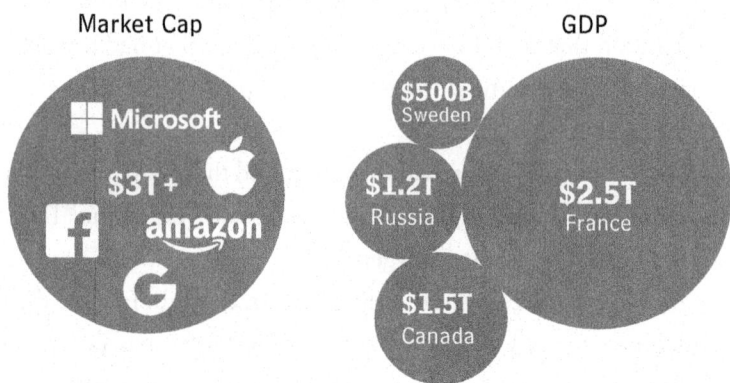

Market Cap

Microsoft
$3T +
amazon
G

GDP

$500B
Sweden
$1.2T
Russia
$2.5T
France
$1.5T
Canada

Taking a worst-case scenario, what if automation can dispossess a significant percentage of the US or world population? What would become of thirty million, three hundred million, or three billion people with neither hope nor prospects for prosperity?

We are so many centuries removed that we have nearly forgotten the word *revolution*, except in the dustbins of history.

But the Innovation Cycle is accelerating. Donald J. Trump is in office in 2017.

Did you think he would be ten years prior? Five years prior? One year prior?

Who will be in the world's offices tomorrow?

Anything is possible today.

In 1776, Adam Smith wrote in *The Wealth of Nations*, "Every individual necessarily labors to render the annual revenue of the society as great as he can.... He intends only his own gain, and he is in this, as in many other cases, led by an invisible hand to promote an end which was no part of his intention."

The end to which Smith refers is the unintended social benefit of broad income distribution resulting from individually self-interested actions. Individual selfishness begets the greater good.

For centuries, the invisible hand has silently set supply and demand and lifted the standard of living, wealth, and prosperity of the rich *and* the poor.

But democracy and capitalism were crafted in a legacy era. They did not anticipate the cycle times of the digital era.

Today, instead of a benign invisible hand, we have a Digital Hand.

The Digital Hand concentrates wealth in the hands of the very, very few, on a scale that will surpass the steel and oil magnates of the industrial era and the financial tycoons of the past and present.

At the same time, it enables the broad-scale automation of jobs, depressing the prospects of the middle classes around the world.

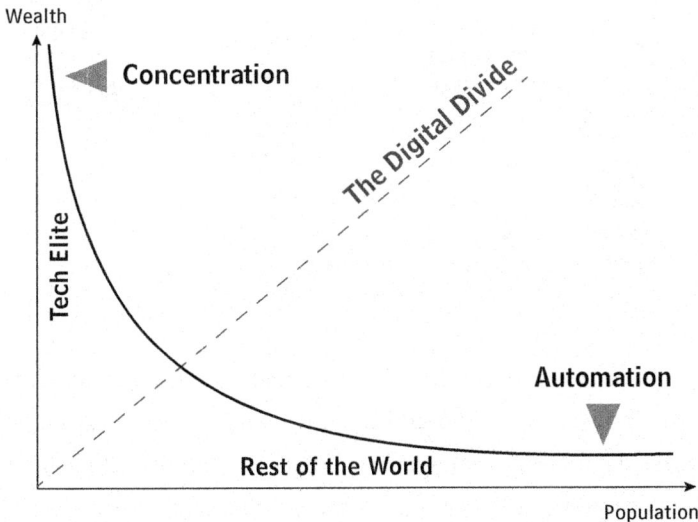

The evaporating middle cannot hold.

In Silicon Valley, there are many who believe the fears of the new Luddites are unfounded, that innovation will surely produce greater wealth and prosperity, opening new avenues for economic gain.

But economic gains are not evenly distributed. There are no giant helicopters filled with cash, distributing wealth evenly around the world. What if those gains are concentrated predominantly in the hands of the tech elite?

Instead of hoping for equal or acceptable wealth distribution, the Tech Titans—the billionaires with the resources and ability to drive change—need to focus on What Is Most Important When.

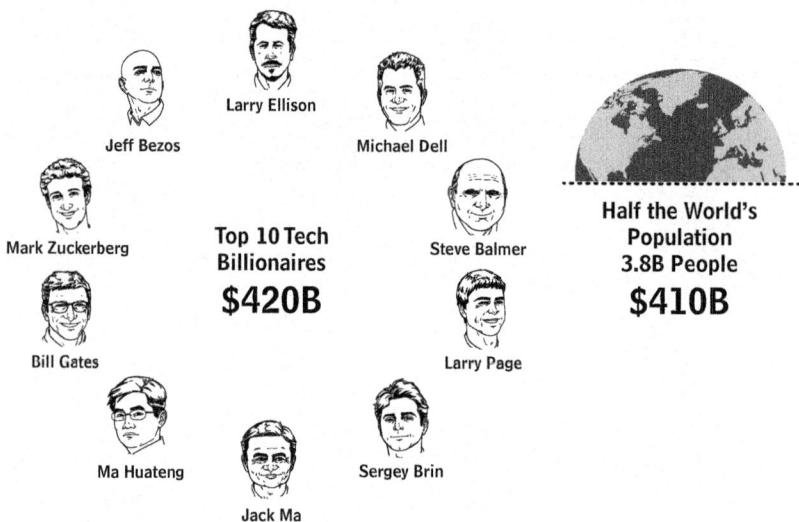

Jeff Bezos
Larry Ellison
Michael Dell
Mark Zuckerberg
Steve Balmer
Bill Gates
Larry Page
Ma Huateng
Sergey Brin
Jack Ma

Top 10 Tech Billionaires
$420B

**Half the World's Population
3.8B People**
$410B

Today, we need sustainable, respectable jobs for middle classes around the world. We need it before we pursue far-flung causes. We need it for long-term global and national stability, which in the long run preserves the ability to pursue all other causes.

Instead of proposing condescending programs such as Universal Basic Income, which appeal to the weakness in human nature, why not build programs that can appeal to the best in human nature? Appeal to the desire to *achieve,* the desire to *contribute.* Enable the continued pursuit of the American dream for the world at large.

Adam Smith warned governments to guard against externalities—the accidental costs of businesses, such as the *Exxon Valdez* oil spill. But what can a government do, or what will a government do, if the externality puts the acting president in office?

After kissing babies on a tour of the fifty United States, Mark Zuckerberg recently changed the mission statement for Facebook. It now reads: "To build community and bring the world closer together."

It's a minor improvement over the prior statement, but Facebook needs more than subtlety to solve its challenges.

So far, we have seen Facebook roll out a fact-checking feature, alerting users to disputed content. In addition, they have added tools to improve groups and make them more meaningful. Administrators can now offer screening quizzes and purge posts from banned members.

Doesn't that allow us to further filter ourselves into 0s and 1s?

Surely there must be more, or are we seeing the negligent efforts of a modern Marie Antoinette? Is the new refrain "Let them eat Internet"?

In his recent commencement speech at Harvard, Zuckerberg said, "Today I want to talk about purpose."

Zuckerberg has achieved the polar opposite of his company's stated purpose.

Instead of purpose, how about taking responsibility for the damaging effects of his platform? How about self-accountability?

You cannot solve externalities of this magnitude with feature tweaks for groups. You cannot delegate social responsibility to algorithms and AI.

And a final warning for the legacy chief: If technology companies can *accidentally* divide nations and destroy social, economic, and political structures that have stood for centuries, how long before an nth-order effect from an Appzilla catches you?

It's time to disrupt or die.

ACKNOWLEDGMENTS

Brett Stevens is a graphics genius. He has the magical ability to take complex inputs and simplify them into easily readable charts. Thank you, Brett, for iterating and finalizing the graphics throughout the book.

Without Tom Foremski, editor of the *Silicon Valley Watcher*, this book would never have been written. Thank you, Tom, for inciting the project and helping me conduct and transcribe several interviews.

Before I wrote the book, I spoke the book. It took a great deal of work listening to the dictations and assembling an initial draft. Thank you, Brooke White, for your patience and perseverance.

We organized the chapters in the book to align with the "innovator's journey." Thank you, Mark Chait, for setting a great framework for the content.

There are several reviewers who helped improve the content and provide endorsements, including Hilary Ahern, Jyoti Bansal, Chad Cardenas, David Castellani, Asheem Chandna, David Cheriton, Roger Dickey, Joanna Doyle, Daniel Freeman, Rick Hopfer, Robert Kraft, Kaycee Lai, Barry Libenson, Joe Lonsdale, Ronnie Lott, Ralph Loura, David McJannet, Jeb Miller, Chris Preimesberger, Chris Schaepe, Dan Scholnick, Frank Slootman,

Scott Spradley, Milo Sprague, Marivi Stuchinksy, and Ed Walsh. While this book represents my views and does not represent the views of Delphix, I'd like to thank Chris Cook, Delphix CEO, for his support throughout the writing process.

Finally, a few reviewers made significant contributions, so a special thank-you to Gene Kim, Ade McCormack, Chris Laping, and Andrew Li.

GLOSSARY

AI: artificial intelligence; computers or technology with the ability to learn from and adapt to their environment or data, divided into two categories: (1) *Narrow AI*, which feeds training data to machine learning, deep learning, and other algorithms to derive computer-generated results, and (2) *Super AI* (also referred to as general AI), which includes self-awareness and self-directed intelligence beyond the narrow scope of training data.

Anti-Diversity Strategy: intentional homogeneity of early founding teams, which reduces the friction from divergent cultural backgrounds to ensure harmony early in a startup's life cycle while pursuing product success; one of the causes of lack of diversity in tech companies; suggests that true, lasting diversity requires a diverse set of successful founding teams.

Anti-Innovator Bias: the tendency to avoid or discount personalities perceived as brash, arrogant, reckless, or otherwise undesirable that may be key to unlocking innovation for a company or industry.

Anti-Leader: the brash, arrogant, reckless, overly aggressive, harsh, or unlikable leaders who often beget beautiful, elegant, and delightful products and many of the world's largest technology companies (e.g., Travis Kalanick, former Uber CEO); the opposite of a humble, enabling, process-driven leader.

APE: Application Platform Ecosystem; a system in which developers and independent software vendors build apps for a platform, increasing the total value of the platform and ecosystem for consumers.

API: Application Programming Interface; a set of tools made available to enable software development, contributing to the rise of *APEs*.

App Solar System (ASS): Application Solar System; a line of products and services developed with interconnected applications (e.g., Apple's Siri, iPods, iPads, Macs, etc.); the new competitive landscape for the most dominant technology companies in the world, including Apple, Alphabet, and Amazon, the ruling aces of the digital era.

Appzilla: an app that grows to gigantic proportions (>$1 billion in revenue or value) and transforms its market, becoming a force in the economy.

Automation Apocalypse: the predicted shift in society as automated systems become more prevalent, eliminating jobs for large populations and challenging the stability of economic and political systems, such as capitalism and democracy.

Blitzscale: a term coined by Reid Hoffman of LinkedIn, where companies scale really quickly for offensive or defensive reasons "with the goal of becoming the first mover at scale," often consuming large amounts of capital to pursue growth at the expense of operational efficiency.

Board Composition: the structure of an organization's board, including number of voting seats controlled by venture capitalists, number of voting seats controlled by founders, member backgrounds, committees, and authority to act.

Bottom-Up Disruption: on the *Tree of Innovation*, bottom-up disruption is a branch where new entrants focus on underserved segments of a market with simpler, easier-to-use solutions, then add features to expand into new segments, eventually moving upmarket and disrupting incumbents.

Branch of Imitation: on the *Tree of Innovation*, this branch comprises companies that take their key ideas directly (as opposed to transference) from other companies (e.g., GUI, mouse, Ethernet taken from Xerox PARC).

Cap Table: capitalization table; a data table delineating percentage and number of shares owned by shareholders of a company across different classes of stock and options, including various prices paid by stakeholders for their securities.

Contribution Paradox: the disproportionate impact (often correlated with ownership stakes) of the few early employees of a company who build the initial product(s) versus the majority of people hired to do the majority of work over time.

Control: the terms, shareholding percentages, and board seat ownership that determine who has the authority to direct an organization toward success (e.g., founders, internal management, or venture capitalists).

Culture: the intangible atmosphere of an organization, often defined as a written set of values or operating principles and highly influenced by a company's vision and mission.

Customer Centered: prioritizing the positive experience of customers, often ahead of profits and what competitors may be offering.

Customer Development: a process developed by Steve Blank, where startups test their product and market hypothesis by "getting out of the office" and meeting with customers to validate product ideas and features; while user and customer validation can be helpful, Customer Development suffers from *Survivorship Bias* and *Small Sample Bias.*

Cyclones: engines of rapid scale for technology companies, including Application Platform Ecosystems (*APEs*), networks, and marketplaces; highly defensible once critical mass is achieved.

Deal Summary: a synopsis of terms for a proposed financing.

Digital Avalanche: the cascade of resources, expertise, and capital that follows the discovery or launch of a revolutionary technology product, which magnifies execution and growth.

Digital Elephants: the uncomfortable and often unspoken truth that most legacy companies say they are focused on digital transformation, but few can demonstrate projects or plans that will truly achieve digital transformation.

Digital Food Chain: a framework for understanding *What Is Most Important When* in the life cycle of a startup; like the biological food chain, each level limits and feeds the next trophic level, starting with market at the base, followed by product, vision, culture, team, strategy, and execution.

Digital Hand: like the "invisible hand" sets market prices in capitalism, the *Digital Hand* is an unseen force that simultaneously concentrates wealth into the hands of the technical elite, while automating away jobs and reducing the prosperity of the many.

Digital Rabbit Hole: a technical opportunity or idea that leads you down the path of digital transformation or into startup land.

Disconfirmation Bias: the tendency to seek out information, sources, or expertise that challenge, reshape, or negate one's beliefs or theories, thereby increasing survivability and durability; the opposite of confirmation bias.

ERP: enterprise resource planning; back-office automation software for business management.

Fair Warning: a kind of company culture that is up front and direct about its policies and expectations to enable like-minded individuals to self-select into an organization and others to self-select out.

Fault Finders: successful, experienced individuals who can critique your ideas and systems of belief, finding faults ahead of time that ultimately save you time and wasted effort.

Feed Addiction Disorder: a global disorder affecting modern societies where algorithms and *AI* in social networking feeds tend to amplify the worst in human nature, virally propagating information that leads to outrage, confirmation bias, or both, polarizing societies and undermining the stability of political institutions and nations; magnified by the vacuum created by the fall of centralized media with responsible editorial boards.

Financial Myopia: the tendency for markets and the financial community to focus on short-term financial metrics in an age where long-term stability can be quickly or instantaneously upended (e.g., Amazon eats Whole Foods for the grocery industry).

Fishes and Whales: the paradox wherein small ideas or ventures look innocuous, like small Fish but quickly grow into technology Whales that can consume industries; also the failure to acquire future Whales when they are Fish-sized due to relatively trivial differences in perceived price and value (e.g., Yahoo's early refusal to buy Google based on price); alternatively, ideas inside of companies that give rise to larger companies outside the originating companies (e.g., the idea for the Slack Whale came from inside a failed Fish, Tiny Speck).

Flywheels: an engine for growth for legacy companies, where the accumulation of product, marketing, sales, and other efforts under a cohesive strategy result in faster and faster momentum and growth.

Framework: a logical structure for supporting knowledge, accelerating learning, enabling quality ideation, making consistent decisions, and so forth; when well documented, shared, and applied, frameworks can drive a cohesive operational culture.

Go-to-Market (GTM) Strategy: how a company intends to package, price, distribute, and deliver products or services to reach customers.

Heuristic: a simple principle or idea to help individuals make decisions or solve problems; when well documented, shared, and applied, heuristics can drive a cohesive operational culture.

Inhibitor Feeders: developments that attack friction points in startups, accelerating the process for all who follow.

Innovation Cycle: the ever-accelerating cycle of inventing technology products, bringing them to market, and scaling their success and impact, ultimately giving rise to the next wave of innovations.

Innovation Glass Ceiling: the false belief that digital innovation is an abstract or complicated goal attainable only by the technical elite, when, in reality, innovation often begins with humble, ordinary ideas accessible to every woman and every man; not to be confused with the glass ceiling of gender inequality.

Innovation Triangle: a framework for fully understanding an innovative idea, comprising the right product, business model, and *go-to-market strategy*; in the digital era, business models and *go-to-market strategies* often have to be built into products, making the three elements of the framework inseparable.

ISVs: independent software vendors; organizations that produce software, often for Application Platform Ecosystems (*APEs*).

Lean: a startup methodology espoused by Eric Ries, where entrepreneurs build a *minimum viable product (MVP)* and create a build-measure-learn feedback loop with validated learning from customers driving product direction and strategy; suffers from *Survivorship Bias* and *Small Sample Bias*.

Levels of UXD: user experience design encompasses all interactions of a user with a company; levels of UXD include products, ecosystems, and all company touchpoints (e.g., sales, marketing, storefronts, etc.).

Liquidation Preferences: the way assets are prioritized for sale during a liquidation process; a key term in startup financing that determines the final outcomes for shareholders of different classes of stock.

Magic Metric: the metric that can guide your product or organization toward exponential growth (e.g., Facebook's seven friends in ten days or Zynga's users who return the day after sign-up).

Marketing Rabbit Hole: the digitization of the many layers of marketing, resulting in an explosion of marketing startups and tools that often require a development background to implement and manage effectively.

MBOs: management by objectives; outlining specific objectives and managing an organization toward those goals, often on an annual basis in private conversations between managers and their direct reports.

Milking Dinosaurs: a strategy for maximizing or preserving revenue from legacy or shrinking products, platforms, ecosystems, or markets, rather than building winning products that will grow in markets of the future.

Minimum Viable Product (MVP): a product with the least risk or cost that will still succeed in the marketplace; see *Lean*.

Narrow AI: machine learning, deep learning, and other artificial intelligence approaches, which use algorithms to process data to derive computer-generated results; can be classified into supervised approaches where targets are predefined and tested against training data, and unsupervised approaches where targets are not predefined.

Nesting Dolls: a branch on the *Tree of Innovation*; like Russian nesting dolls of decreasing sizes that nestle within one another, technology products, services, and platforms can do the same, each new development fitting within another or fitting outside another, resulting in smaller and larger systems.

OKRs: objectives and key results; a framework for achieving goals by which objectives are set and progress is measured in key results; unlike *MBOs*, OKRs are often shared openly across an organization, reviewed weekly, and set quarterly.

Omni-Channel: a marketing and sales strategy that spans all available channels for customers to make purchases, including mobile devices, Internet browsers, physical stores, and so on.

Ownership Triangle: nestled within the *Innovation Triangle*; the composition of terms, board members, and *cap table* to determine ownership for a startup.

Pay to Grow: investing large amounts of capital in order to drive sales, often at the expense of short-term and possibly long-term operational efficiency.

Perpetual Model: a pricing strategy with an up-front fee that grants perpetual rights to licensed software, often accompanied by an annual maintenance fee typically in the range of 20 percent of the up-front fee.

Pied Pipers: dynamic personalities that can engage talented people in challenging missions to win markets and possibly change the world.

Platform Convergence: a branch on the *Tree of Innovation*; when a new technology platform emerges, niches filled by apps in other platforms are filled by similar apps in the new platform, converging in features and functions across platforms.

PMF: Product-Market Fit; whether a product meets its determined market's demands or, conversely, whether there is a sufficient and waiting market for a given product.

Product Trinity: key roles in the digital era, including product manager, chief technology officer, and the head of user experience design; often the CEOs of technology companies embody and operate in all three capacities.

Quality Tail: the quality required for a product to reliably support a market of customers at varying degrees of a startup's scale.

Race to Zero: the strategy by which an organization vies for control at the lowest end of the value chain, then commoditizes higher elements of the value chain to drive revenues and margins (e.g., Amazon combined data centers and computer hardware, at the low end of the value chain, into a set of services that enabled cloud computing; now they provide increasingly sophisticated software offerings that commoditize products further up the value chain).

Regional Convergence: a branch of the *Tree of Innovation*; when a geographical region has sufficient isolation (e.g., the Great Firewall of China), apps evolve to fill niches in the isolated region that are similar to or imitate apps in other regions, converging in features and functions across regions.

Riding Elephants: a *go-to-market strategy* where startups take their products to market by leveraging the reach and customer install base of a much larger organization (e.g., IBM ceding the personal computer operating system to Microsoft, making it the de facto operating system of the personal computer era).

Rocket Builders: the early employees of a startup who define and build a successful product and often define the business model and a repeatable *go-to-market strategy* (e.g., Google's founders working from their garage).

Rocket Riders: employees who join after a successful product has been built and contribute to the ongoing success and direction of the organization but do not necessarily know how to build the rocket ship or set the preconditions necessary to enable a significant success (e.g., Marissa Mayer, an early employee at Google who failed to define a winning strategy as CEO of Yahoo).

SaaS: software-as-a-service; centrally hosted software provided to consumers as a subscription-based service.

Sales Before Expense: a timeless rule of business where you spend less money than you can bring in from sales.

SAM: Serviceable Available Market; the portion of total market that is within an organization's geographical or platform reach; a subset of Total Available Market (*TAM*).

Separation of Users and Buyers: a service that is free to users but funded in other ways, such as advertising, so that the app or platform's market of buyers is not the same as its market of users; enables the fast increase of users and company value, often in advance of sales and revenue growth.

Series FF Stock: named for the Founders Fund, Series FF is a special class of common stock, sometimes granted to founders, that

can be sold and converted to preferred stock at a later financing
round if purchased at the same price as preferred shares (i.e., it
allows a founder to sell some shares at preferred prices at later
financing rounds, after a company has appreciated in value but
before an IPO).

Skinner Boxes: a chamber with a method to reward (food) and punish
(electrocution) designed to test rat behavior, which uncovered
that intermittent rewards have great motivational power; refers
to B. F. Skinner's punishment and reward research.

Small Sample Bias: an error where the sample of user or customer
feedback does not represent the general population or market,
often due to lack of access to a large-enough sample.

SOM: Serviceable Obtainable Market; the portion of your geographically available or platform available market you can capture,
especially in the short term; a subset of Serviceable Available
Market (*SAM*).

Subscription Model: recurring payments for access to a product
or service.

Success Fallacy: the misconception that executives and employees of
successful technology companies can replicate their success in
other environments, especially when applied to *Rocket Riders*,
who can tell detailed stories of the path to success but may have
been successful due to the system and preconditions around them
rather than their own actions and abilities.

Super AI: self-aware and self-directed artificial intelligence, which can generate results, thoughts, or actions beyond the narrow scope of training data; popularized in science fiction novels and movies, such as Skynet in *The Terminator*, which successfully eradicates the majority of humankind; also referred to as general AI.

Survivorship Bias: a logical error made by focusing on people, products, startups, or things that survive while overlooking the characteristics of those that failed; when applied to *Lean*, it is the logical error of overlooking all the startups that built minimum viable products, engaged customers for validation, made pivots, and still failed.

Systems Map: a visual and logical depiction of the components of a system or process; a visual depiction of components of app systems, with apps at the top, supported by databases, software platforms, and hardware platforms on the bottom.

Talent Trunk: the foundation for the *Tree of Innovation*; talent supports and weaves through all other branches of innovation.

TAM: Total Available Market; the complete market that exists for a product, regardless of accessibility; a superset of Serviceable Available Market (*SAM*) and Serviceable Obtainable Market (*SOM*).

Tech Dinosaurs: large technology companies with declining user bases of their once-dominant platforms and systems, including IBM, HP, Dell, Oracle, and Microsoft.

Tech Superpowers: the five largest and most powerful companies in the tech industry, which have also been the five largest companies by market capitalization in the world in 2017—Apple, Alphabet, Amazon, Facebook, and Microsoft.

Tech Tax: the exorbitant cost of living in the Bay Area due to high salaries, wealth generated from successful technology companies, and cities that house relatively small populations; results in incredible housing prices and a dramatic compression of disposable income.

Technology Transfer: a branch of the *Tree of Innovation*; applying an existing technology from one market to a new product in a new market or niche, often adding different features, packaging, or pricing to serve the new market or niche.

Tech Titans: founders, CEOs, and executives of technology companies who have generated at least $1 billion in personal net worth, with the power, resources, and ability to make a lasting impact on the world.

Thinking Big and Small: a parallel to Daniel Kahneman's *Thinking, Fast and Slow*; the innovator thinks in both large scale about markets and in fine details about technology and products to ensure logical *Product-Market Fit*, resulting in a clear product vision.

Tree of Innovation: the digital equivalent of Darwin's radiation of species, also known as the Tree of Life; the map of innovation into branches of parents and descendants; the foundation is the *Talent Trunk* and branches include *Bottom-up Disruption, Imitation, Platform Convergence, Regional Convergence, Technology Transfer,* and *Nesting Dolls*.

Unintended Polar Consequences: the potential for technology leaders or companies to achieve the opposite of their intended mission or effects; results from the unpredictability of technology's impact on markets, economic and political systems, and nations.

Use Cases: a series of interactions for a user of a product to achieve a specific goal (e.g., a consumer goes onto the Amazon website, browses for books, buys a physical book, and has it delivered to her door); defining use cases is a key element of *Thinking Big and Small* and ensuring clarity of product vision.

UXD: user experience design; the design factors that make products or services usable, accessible, and enjoyable for end users; see *Levels of UXD*.

V2MOM: Vision, Values, Methods, Obstacles, and Measures; the management framework used by Marc Benioff at Salesforce.com.

Value Seams: the holes that develop in existing markets and provide opportunity for innovation; a critical component of Thinking Big, which encompasses understanding changes in market dynamics, user pain points, and the potential value of an innovation; see *Thinking Big and Small.*

Value Triangle: a simple framework for judging the worth of potential innovation against three factors—market size, time to value, and value differential; for innovation to be worth pursuing (except for small, lifestyle businesses intended to make a living), innovation should fall into the following acceptance ranges: $100 million to >$100 billion for market size, 1 second to 1 year for time to value, and 1x to >1,000x for value differential.

VSE: Vision, Strategy, and Execution; the management framework used by John Chambers of Cisco.

Weeds Versus Seeds: the paradox that the leaders of the world's largest technology companies spend significant amounts of time managing Seeds—reviewing technology details, product definition, and user experience design (see *Product Trinity*)—compared to CEOs of legacy companies who feel such detail work is too trivial, or in the Weeds, for management at scale.

WIMIW: What Is Most Important When; prioritization in the life of a startup; see *Digital Food Chain*.

RESOURCES

INTRODUCTION

Uber Newsroom: https://newsroom.uber.com/ubers-founding/

Uber Website: https://www.uber.com/our-story/

Get Paid for Your Pad Website: https://getpaidforyourpad.com/
blog/the-airbnb-founder-story/

TechCrunch: https://techcrunch.com/
gallery/a-brief-history-of-snapchat/slide/8/

Inc.: https://www.inc.com/business-insider/snapchat-ceo-
founder-evan-spiegel-fabulous-life-story.html

Forbes: https://www.forbes.com/sites/jjcolao/2014/01/06/
the-inside-story-of-snapchat-the-worlds-hottest-app-or-a-
3-billion-disappearing-act/2/#78d54cb1d017

The Harvard Crimson: https://www.the-
crimson.com/article/2004/6/10/
mark-e-zuckerberg-06-the-whiz/?page=single

CHAPTER 1: I SEE DEAD COMPANIES

The Wall Street Journal: https://www.wsj.com/articles/u-s-bank-
ing-industry-annual-profit-hit-record-in-2016-1488295836

Morgan Stanley Website: https://www.morganstanley.com/
articles/autonomous-cars-the-future-is-now

Fast Company: https://www.fastcompany.com/3026418/
   this-story-about-slacks-founder-says-everything-you-need-
   to-know-about-him
Startup Grind on Medium: https://medium.com/startup-grind/
   growing-as-fast-as-slack-195c1e194561
Visual Capitalist: https://www.visualcapitalist.com/
   extraordinary-size-amazon-one-chart/
Wikipedia: https://en.wikipedia.org/wiki/
   Slack_(software)#cite_note-Koetsier-18
TechCrunch: https://techcrunch.com/2016/10/20/slunk/
Business Insider: http://www.businessinsider.com/intercom-is-
   on-track-to-be-one-of-the-fastest-growing-startups-2017-2

CHAPTER 2: THINKING BIG AND SMALL

Forbes: https://www.forbes.com/sites/jjcolao/2014/01/06/
   the-inside-story-of-snapchat-the-worlds-hottest-app-or-a-
   3-billion-disappearing-act/2/#78d54cb1d017
Harvard Business Review: https://hbr.org/2013/05/
   why-the-lean-start-up-changes-everything
Steve Blank Website: https://steveblank.com/about/
CB Insights: https://www.cbinsights.com/blog/
   venture-capital-funnel-2/

CHAPTER 3: THE INNOVATION TRIANGLE

Fortune: http://fortune.com/2014/01/23/
   lessons-from-the-death-of-a-tech-goliath/
Behind the Cloud, by Marc Benioff

CHAPTER 4: THE VALUE TRIANGLE

Deutsche Welle: http://www.dw.com/en/von-bechtolsheim-i-
invested-in-google-to-solve-my-own-problem/a-4557608

Forbes: https://www.forbes.com/profile/
andreas-von-bechtolsheim/

CHAPTER 5: LEARNING SLOW AND FAST

Reddit: https://www.reddit.com/r/IAmA/comments/2rgsan/i_
am_elon_musk_ceocto_of_a_rocket_company_ama/

CHAPTER 6: DISCONFIRMATION BIAS

Mental Floss: http://mentalfloss.com/article/71643/15-things-
you-might-not-know-about-michelangelos-david

USA Today: https://www.usatoday.com/story/
money/personalfinance/2014/08/24/
peculiar-habits-of-successful-people/14447531/

All Things D: http://allthingsd.com/20120529/
steve-jobs-was-an-awesome-flip-flopper-says-tim-cook/

Amazon Website: https://www.amazon.jobs/principles

Signal v. Noise: https://signalvnoise.com/
posts/3289-some-advice-from-jeff-bezos

CHAPTER 7: THE TREE OF INNOVATION

Wikipedia: https://en.wikipedia.org/wiki/
Great_American_Interchange

TechCrunch: https://techcrunch.com/2016/06/24/
why-a-palantir-ipo-might-not-be-far-off/

Zero to One, by Peter Thiel

Business Insider: http://www.businessinsider.com/
meet-the-paypal-mafia-the-richest-group-of-men-in-sili-
con-valley-2014-9

Network World: http://www.networkworld.com/article/2254433/
virtualization/with-long-history-of-virtualization-behind-
it--ibm-looks-to-the-future.html

SparkNotes: http://www.sparknotes.com/biology/evolution/pat-
ternsofevolution/section1.rhtml

CNN: http://money.cnn.com/interactive/technology/china-
apps/index.html

Folklore.org: http://www.folklore.org/StoryView.py?story=A_
Rich_Neighbor_Named_Xerox.txt

New York Times: http://www.nytimes.com/2009/07/09/technol-
ogy/companies/09data.html

CHAPTER 8: VISION

Forbes: https://www.forbes.com/sites/joannmuller/2017/05/21/
ford-fires-ceo-mark-fields-former-steelcase-chief-jim-hack-
ett-to-take-over/#3e2e51c679dc

Outliers, by Malcolm Gladwell

Elon Musk: Tesla, SpaceX, and the Quest for a Fantastic Future,
by Ashlee Vance

CHAPTER 9: LEADERS AND ANTI-LEADERS

Business Insider: http://www.businessinsider.com/
what-warren-buffett-looks-for-in-candidates-2017-1

Jalopnik: https://jalopnik.com/ubers-internal-investigation-
reveals-its-everything-you-1796065030

Business Insider: http://www.businessinsider.com/
　　how-mark-zuckerberg-booted-his-co-founder-out-of-the-
　　company-2012-5
USA Today Sports: http://ftw.usatoday.com/2017/01/
　　san-francisco-49ers-chip-kelly-fired-trent-baalke-head-
　　coach-search-worst-woner-nfl
Google+: https://plus.google.com/+RipRowan/posts/
　　eVeouesvaVX

CHAPTER 10: BUILT TO FAIL

Fortune: http://fortune.com/2016/03/21/
　　andy-grove-fortune-classic/
CNBC: http://www.cnbc.com/2017/06/16/whole-foods-ceo-
　　once-called-amazons-grocery-delivery-service-its-waterloo.
　　html
Quora: https://www.quora.com/In-Tesla-and-SpaceX-how-
　　much-of-the-technical-designing-is-Elon-Musk-involved-in
CNBC: http://www.cnbc.com/2017/06/16/after-its-stock-pop-
　　amazon-will-get-whole-foods-essentially-for-free.html
YouTube: https://www.youtube.com/watch?v=djB6BmBda6Q
Fortune: http://fortune.com/2017/06/12/ge-stock-jeff-immelt/
Fortune: http://fortune.com/2017/05/25/
　　jeff-immelt-places-big-bets-on-ges-software-push/
Fortune: http://fortune.com/2016/11/15/ges-ceo-digital-remake/
Business Insider: http://www.businessinsider.com/
　　ge-ceo-jeff-immelt-top-10-software-company-2015-9

CHAPTER 11: DIGITAL FOOD CHAIN

Slate: http://www.slate.com/blogs/future_tense/2014/11/03/
larry_page_says_that_google_needs_to_move_on_from_
its_don_t_be_evil_mission.html

Wikipedia: https://en.wikipedia.org/wiki/Food_chain

YouTube: https://www.youtube.com/watch?v=EFWG51nGmGA

Facebook Website: https://www.facebook.com/pg/facebook/
about/

I Done This Blog: http://blog.idonethis.com/one-thing-extreme-
focus-facebook-mark-zuckerberg-paypal-peter-thiel/

The Harvard Crimson: https://www.the-
crimson.com/article/2004/6/10/
mark-e-zuckerberg-06-the-whiz/?page=single

Fast Company: https://www.fastcompany.com/3033427/
hit-the-ground-running/what-happens-after-you-get-shot-
down-by-mark-zuckerberg

CHAPTER 12: CULTURE

Bible

CHAPTER 13: TEAM

Wikipedia: https://en.wikipedia.org/wiki/Marissa_Mayer

Simply Safe Dividends: https://www.simplysafedividends.com/
warren-buffett-investment-advice/

New York Times: https://www.nytimes.com/2017/06/03/technol-
ogy/yahoo-marissa-mayer-compensation.html

New York Times: https://www.nytimes.com/2017/06/13/technol-
ogy/yahoo-verizon-marissa-mayer.html

The Everything Store, by Brad Stone

CHAPTER 14: COMPETITION

Goodreads: https://www.goodreads.com/quotes/538257-if-we-
 can-keep-our-competitors-focused-on-us-while
Forbes: https://www.forbes.com/sites/
 stuartanderson/2016/03/26/jyoti-bansal-waited-
 7-years-for-a-green-card-to-start-his-1-9-billion-
 company/#50e4c8876e16

CHAPTER 15: LOW-GROUND STRATEGY

Bloomberg: https://www.bloomb-
 erg.com/news/articles/2016-05-18/
 this-5-billion-software-company-has-no-sales-staff
Wells Fargo Securities Equity Research report on Red Hat, Inc.,
 January 10, 2017

CHAPTER 16: THE MARKETING RABBIT HOLE

Wikipedia: https://en.wikipedia.org/wiki/John_Wanamaker
Alice-in-wonderland.net: http://www.alice-in-wonderland.net/
 resources/chapters-script/alices-adventures-in-wonderland/
Rob Sobers Blog: https://robsobers.
 com/9-dollar-marketing-stack-step-by-step-setup-guide/

CHAPTER 17: EXECUTION

The Guardian US: https://www.theguardian.com/sport/2017/
 apr/21/moneyball-baseball-oakland-book-billy-beane
International Business Times: http://www.ibtimes.com/
 amazon-nearly-20-years-business-it-still-doesnt-make-
 money-investors-dont-seem-care-1513368
Harvard Business Review: https://hbr.org/2016/04/
 blitzscaling#comment-section

Delphix Website: https://www.delphix.com/news/news-release/
    drinks-giant-sabmiller-serves-sap-data-60-times-faster-
    delphix-data-service
Business Insider: http://www.businessinsider.com/
    atlassian-ceo-mike-cannon-brookes-accel-partners-2016-9
Fortune: http://fortune.com/2015/07/29/github-raises-250-mil-
    lion-in-new-funding-now-valued-at-2-billion/
Fortune: http://fortune.com/2015/09/30/
    jack-dorsey-twitter-ceo-fired/
Business Insider: http://www.businessinsider.com/
    github-the-full-inside-story-2016-2
BuzzFeed: https://www.buzzfeed.com/charliewarzel/whats-
    going-on-at-medium?utm_term=.mfwmd04e#.aorvx2Oz
KPCB Website: http://www.kpcb.com/partner/john-doerr
BetterWorks Blog: https://blog.betterworks.com/
    how-google-grew/
Mode Blog: https://blog.modeanalytics.com/
    facebook-aha-moment-simpler-than-you-think/
YouTube: https://www.youtube.com/watch?v=raIUQP71SBU&fe
    ature=youtu.be&t=21m5s (20:45)
First Round Review: http://firstround.com/review/From-0-to-
    1B-Slacks-Founder-Shares-Their-Epic-Launch-Strategy/
GrowHack: http://www.growhack.com/2012/12/
    discovering-your-aha-moment/
Greylock Perspectives: https://news.greylock.com/the-only-
    metric-that-matters-now-with-fancy-slides-232474cf414c
Harvard Business Review: https://hbr.org/2016/04/blitzscaling

CHAPTER 18: PLANET OF THE APES

SDxCentral: https://www.sdxcentral.com/articles/news/
sources-microsoft-tried-to-buy-docker-for-4b/2016/06/

Daily Beast: http://www.thedailybeast.com/
microsoft-ceo-steve-ballmer-to-resign

New York Times: http://www.nytimes.com/2000/04/04/
business/us-vs-microsoft-overview-us-judge-says-micro-
soft-violated-antitrust-laws-with.html

Wikipedia: https://en.wikipedia.org/wiki/
Open-source_software_movement

GNU Operating System Blog: https://www.gnu.org/philosophy/
open-source-misses-the-point.en.html

Wikipedia: https://en.wikipedia.org/wiki/Richard_Stallman

Wikipedia: https://en.wikipedia.org/wiki/
GNU_General_Public_License

The Linux Daily: http://www.thelinuxdaily.com/2010/04/
the-first-linux-announcement-from-linus-torvalds/

YouTube: https://www.youtube.com/watch?v=UOEFXaWHppE

The Art of War, by Sun Tzu

CHAPTER 19: FISHES AND WHALES

Wikipedia: https://en.wikipedia.org/wiki/Palantir_Technologies

BGR: https://bgr.com/2016/12/29/
facebook-instagram-acquisition-1-billion-genius/

Walmart News: https://news.walmart.com/2016/08/08/
walmart-agrees-to-acquire-jetcom-one-of-the-fastest-grow-
ing-e-commerce-companies-in-the-us

AdvertisingAge: http://adage.com/article/digital/
facebook-q4-2016-earnings/302378/

Business Insider: https://www.businessinsider.com.au/

facebook-is-selling-just-4-of-the-company-for-2x-as-much-
as-yahoo-could-have-paid-to-buy-the-whole-thing-2011-
1#in-june-2004-an-unnamed-financier-offered-10-million-1
Fast Company: https://www.fastcompany.com/3028244/
facebook-acquires-oculus-vr-for-2-billion
Business Insider: http://www.businessinsider.com/
whatsapp-facebooks-22-billion-acquisition-did-102-mil-
lion-in-revenue-last-year-2014-10
TechCrunch: https://techcrunch.com/2017/07/26/
slack-is-raising-a-250-million-round-at-5-billion-valuation/
Wikipedia: https://en.wikipedia.org/wiki/History_of_Yahoo!

CHAPTER 20: CYCLONIC FORCES

YouTube: https://www.youtube.com/watch?v=--APdD6vejI:58

AFTERWORD: THE AUTOMATION APOCALYPSE

Visual Capitalist: http://www.visualcapitalist.com/
chart-5-tech-giants-make-billions/
Statistics Times: http://statisticstimes.com/economy/projected-
world-gdp-ranking.php
The New Yorker: http://www.newyo-
rker.com/magazine/2017/05/29/
james-mattis-a-warrior-in-washington
Ian C. Friedman Website: http://www.iancfriedman.com/?p=383
euronews.: http://www.euronews.com/2017/02/09/
what-do-we-know-about-marine-le-pen-s-policies
Wikipedia: https://en.wikipedia.org/wiki/
Theresa_May#Political_positions
The Telegraph: http://www.telegraph.co.uk/news/0/
theresa-may-profile-britains-prime-minister/

BBC.com: http://www.bbc.com/news/uk-politics-36660372

Wikipedia: https://en.wikipedia.org/wiki/Timeline_of_Facebook

Wikipedia: https://en.wikipedia.org/wiki/Invisible_hand

The Guardian US: https://www.theguard-
ian.com/technology/2017/mar/22/
facebook-fact-checking-tool-fake-news

Time: http://time.com/4795031/mark-zuckerberg-facebook-
harvard-commencement-transcript/

Forbes: https://www.forbes.com/richest-in-tech/#a81c17073167

The Guardian US: https://www.theguardian.com/
global-development/2017/jan/16/worlds-eight-richest-peo-
ple-have-same-wealth-as-poorest-50

Business Insider: http://www.businessinsider.com/
richest-people-in-tech-2016-1/#13-jun-lei-1

CPSIA information can be obtained
at www.ICGtesting.com
Printed in the USA
LVOW13*2325301017
554270LV00010BA/113/P